Black Kiss 2

HOWARD CHAYKIN

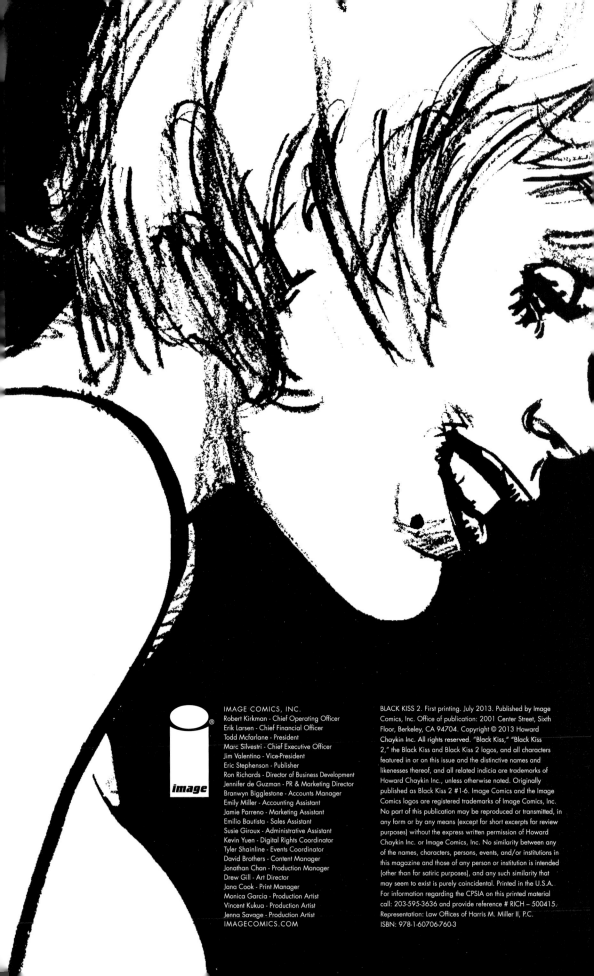

IMAGE COMICS, INC.
Robert Kirkman - Chief Operating Officer
Erik Larsen - Chief Financial Officer
Todd Mcfarlane - President
Marc Silvestri - Chief Executive Officer
Jim Valentino - Vice-President
Eric Stephenson - Publisher
Ron Richards - Director of Business Development
Jennifer de Guzman - PR & Marketing Director
Branwyn Bigglestone - Accounts Manager
Emily Miller - Accounting Assistant
Jamie Parreno - Marketing Assistant
Emilio Bautista - Sales Assistant
Susie Giroux - Administrative Assistant
Kevin Yuen - Digital Rights Coordinator
Tyler Shainline - Events Coordinator
David Brothers - Content Manager
Jonathan Chan - Production Manager
Drew Gill - Art Director
Jana Cook - Print Manager
Monica Garcia - Production Artist
Vincent Kukua - Production Artist
Jenna Savage - Production Artist
IMAGECOMICS.COM

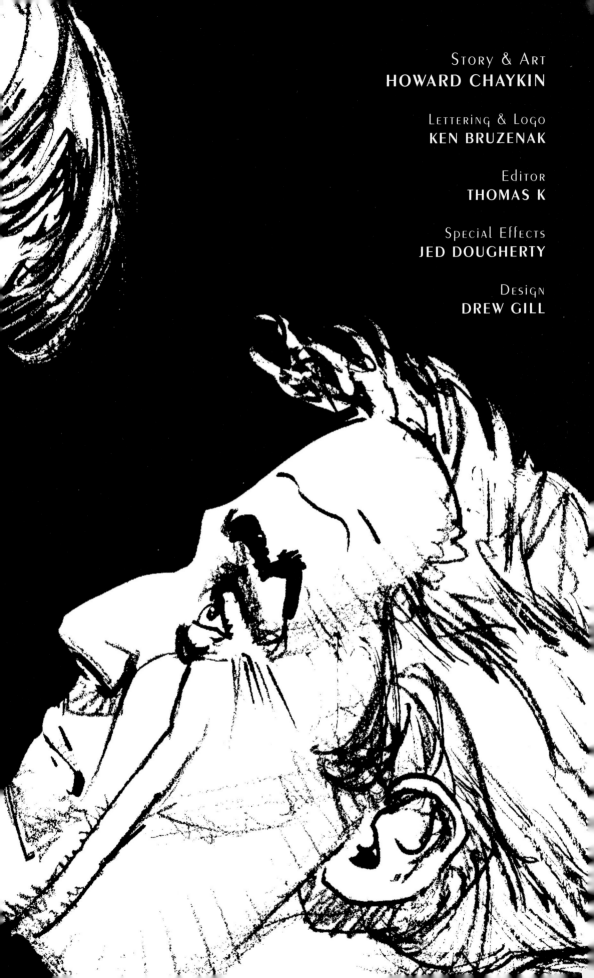

Story & Art
HOWARD CHAYKIN

Lettering & Logo
KEN BRUZENAK

Editor
THOMAS K

Special Effects
JED DOUGHERTY

Design
DREW GILL

Summer, 1906.
New York City.
The Lower East Side of Manhattan.
THE CITY SWELTERS FROM THE BATTERY TO WASHINGTON HEIGHTS...
...THE HEAT RAISING A STENCH OF ROTTING FLORA, DYING FAUNA AND SWEATING, FUCKING AND SHITTING HUMANITY...
...THAT SEEMS TO UNITE EVERY NEIGHBORHOOD IN AN OVER-WHELMING EFFLUVIA OF STINK.
THE BURGHERS UPTOWN...
NICKELODEON
...THE ONES WHO CAN CLAIM TO HAVE FOUND A FOOTHOLD IN THE NEW WORLD ONE, TWO, FIVE, TEN GENERATIONS BACK...
...CAN FOOL THEMSELVES AND THEIR FELLOWS THAT IT'S THE IMMIGRANTS...
NICKELODEON
...THE MICKS, THE MOCKIES, THE DAGOS, THE SPICS...
...WHO ARE STINKING UP THE STREETS OF LITTLE OLD NEW YORK.
COMPLETE AND UTTER BULLSHIT.

ROSE...
...I AIN'T BEEN ABLE TO THINK ABOUT NOTHIN' BUT YER KNISH SINCE I SMELT IT.
SHUT UP AND KEEP FUCKIN', YA SHEENIE BASTARD...
WHIRRRRRRRRRR
ABIE GELBFEIN HAS NO INTENTION OF MAKING AN HONEST WOMAN OF ROSE O'MALLEY...
...MORE COCK, LESS MOUT'.
'S' NOT WHAT YEZ SAID LAS' NIGHT WHEN I HAD MY FACE IN YA LAP.
WHIRRRRRRRRRRR
...AND ROSE WOULD NO MORE BRING THIS HORSECOCKED LITTLE JEW HOME TO HER PARENTS THAN SHE WOULD SUCK THE MONSIGNOR'S COCK...
...AGAIN.
AN' IF YA WANT MY FACE IN YER LAP AGAIN, YE'LL SHUT UP AN' FUCK.
DO ALL IRISH GIRLS TALK SO DOITY?
ONLY THE ONES'RE GOIN'A HELL...
ON THE OTHER HAND, THAT CUTE NEW PRIEST AT St. MARY'S LOOKS LIKE A GOOD RIDE...
...NOW WHAT'D I SAY ABOUT SHUTTIN' UP AN' GETTIN' ON WITH IT?

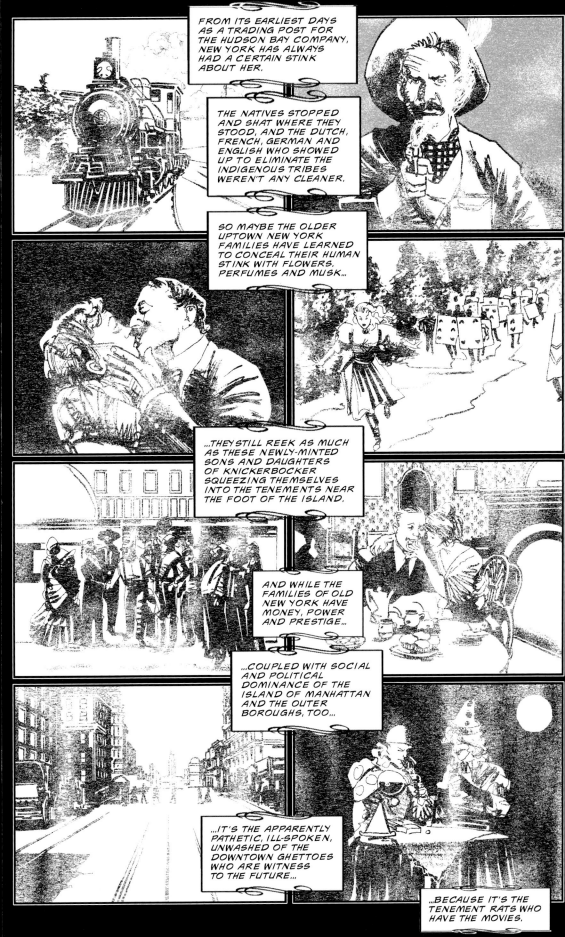

FROM ITS EARLIEST DAYS AS A TRADING POST FOR THE HUDSON BAY COMPANY, NEW YORK HAS ALWAYS HAD A CERTAIN STINK ABOUT HER.

THE NATIVES STOPPED AND SHAT WHERE THEY STOOD, AND THE DUTCH, FRENCH, GERMAN AND ENGLISH WHO SHOWED UP TO ELIMINATE THE INDIGENOUS TRIBES WEREN'T ANY CLEANER.

SO MAYBE THE OLDER UPTOWN NEW YORK FAMILIES HAVE LEARNED TO CONCEAL THEIR HUMAN STINK WITH FLOWERS, PERFUMES AND MUSK...

...THEY STILL REEK AS MUCH AS THESE NEWLY-MINTED SONS AND DAUGHTERS OF KNICKERBOCKER SQUEEZING THEMSELVES INTO THE TENEMENTS NEAR THE FOOT OF THE ISLAND.

AND WHILE THE FAMILIES OF OLD NEW YORK HAVE MONEY, POWER AND PRESTIGE...

...COUPLED WITH SOCIAL AND POLITICAL DOMINANCE OF THE ISLAND OF MANHATTAN AND THE OUTER BOROUGHS, TOO...

...IT'S THE APPARENTLY PATHETIC, ILL-SPOKEN, UNWASHED OF THE DOWNTOWN GHETTOES WHO ARE WITNESS TO THE FUTURE...

...BECAUSE IT'S THE TENEMENT RATS WHO HAVE THE MOVIES.

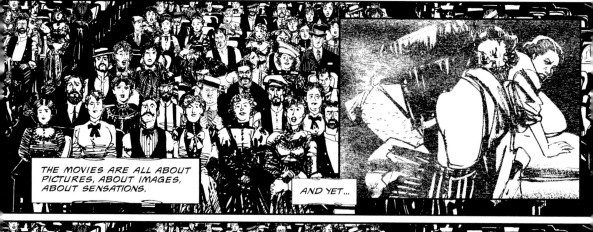

THE MOVIES ARE ALL ABOUT PICTURES, ABOUT IMAGES, ABOUT SENSATIONS.

AND YET...

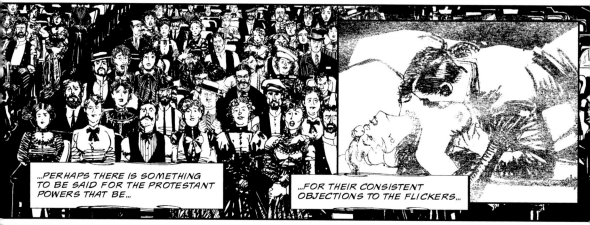

...PERHAPS THERE IS SOMETHING TO BE SAID FOR THE PROTESTANT POWERS THAT BE...

...FOR THEIR CONSISTENT OBJECTIONS TO THE FLICKERS...

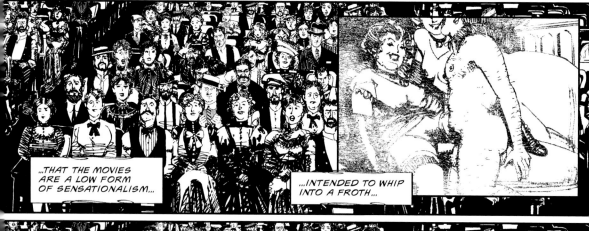

...THAT THE MOVIES ARE A LOW FORM OF SENSATIONALISM...

...INTENDED TO WHIP INTO A FROTH...

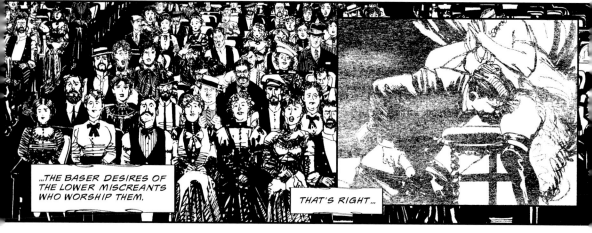

...THE BASER DESIRES OF THE LOWER MISCREANTS WHO WORSHIP THEM.

THAT'S RIGHT...

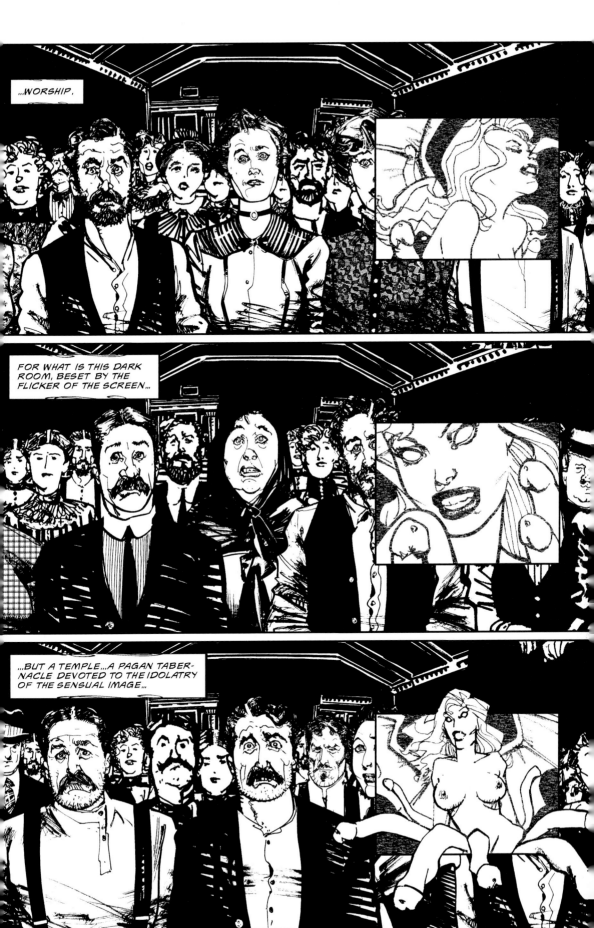

...WORSHIP.

FOR WHAT IS THIS DARK ROOM, BESET BY THE FLICKER OF THE SCREEN...

...BUT A TEMPLE...A PAGAN TABER-NACLE DEVOTED TO THE IDOLATRY OF THE SENSUAL IMAGE...

...APPEALING TO THE DARKER NEEDS OF THE LOWER ORDERS...
...SERVING TO SATISFY THE PRIMAL NEED FOR SHAME AND LUST, GUILT AND FEAR.
SO IT IS WITH THIS CATHEDRAL FLICKERING FROM LIGHT TO DARK...
...YES AND NO...
...GOOD AND EVIL...
...GOD AND LUCIFER...
...SEX AND DEATH.

SCREAMS OF TERROR.
SHRIEKS OF AGONY.
OR ARE THEY MOANS OF PASSION...
...SQUEALS OF SHEER, UNBRIDLED DELIGHT...
...SIGHS OF UTTER SURRENDER TO PLEASURE...
...SHUDDERING GASPS OF THE CLIMB TOWARD CLIMAX...

...AS A COMMUNAL
ORGASM DEVOURS
AND CONSUMES
THIS CONGREGATION
OF SUPPLICANTS...
...TO THE RHYTHMIC
FLUTTER OF THIS
DEITY OF BLACK
AND WHITE...
...THIS TWO-
FACED GOD
OF CINEMA.

NICKELODEON
AN HOUR'S ENTERTAINMENT...
NICKELODEON
...AN HOUR'S RESPITE FROM THE SHORT, BRUTAL ASSAULT THAT IS THEIR LIVES.
BUT TODAY, IN THAT HOUR...
NICKELODEON
...SO UNLIKE THOSE OTHER HOURS IN THE DARK, OF ESCAPE FROM HUMDRUM CARE...
NICKELODEON

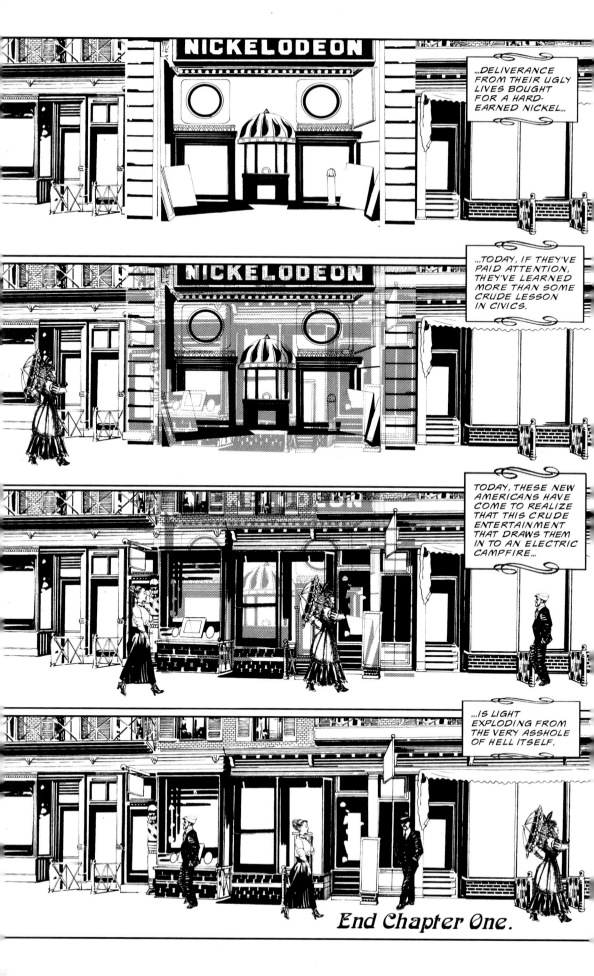

...DELIVERANCE FROM THEIR UGLY LIVES BOUGHT FOR A HARD-EARNED NICKEL...

...TODAY, IF THEY'VE PAID ATTENTION, THEY'VE LEARNED MORE THAN SOME CRUDE LESSON IN CIVICS.

TODAY, THESE NEW AMERICANS HAVE COME TO REALIZE THAT THIS CRUDE ENTERTAINMENT THAT DRAWS THEM IN TO AN ELECTRIC CAMPFIRE...

...IS LIGHT EXPLODING FROM THE VERY ASSHOLE OF HELL ITSELF.

End Chapter One.

SPRING, 1912.
THE NORTH ATLANTIC.
"Oh they built the ship Titanic, for to sail the ocean blue...
"...and they thought they had a ship that the water wouldn't go through...
"...husbands and wives, little children lost their lives...
"...it was sad when the great ship went down."
CHARLIE KEATON...?
KENTON--
CHARLIE KENTON.

CHARLES KENTON.
'CHARLIE' TO HIS FRIENDS.
'BUBBA' TO HIS INTIMATE FRIENDS.
CHARLIE IS A 20 YEAR-OLD VIRGIN...
...MINUTES AWAY FROM LOSING HIS PURITY...
MOVE IT ALONG, DEARIE, WE AIN'T GOT ALL NIGHT.
...AND GAINING A VENEREAL DISEASE...
...BUT SOMEWHERE, THERE ARE TWIN GODS WITH OTHER PLANS.
"It was midnight on the sea, the band was playing 'Nearer my God to thee'...

"...fare thee, Titanic, fare thee well.
"Jack Johnson wanna get on board...
"...the Cap'n says ' we don't haul no coal' ...
"...fare thee, Titanic, fare thee well."
BUBBA'S BEEN TRYING TO LOSE HIS VIRGINITY SINCE HE LEFT THE COTSWOLDS A YEAR AGO.

NOW HE'S GOING TO DIE, UNSULLIED AND INNOCENT.
FOR AS LONG AS HE CAN RECALL, ALL HE'S EVER WANTED WERE TWO THINGS.
A MOIST QUIM TO REPLACE HIS SPIT-WET RIGHT HAND...
...AND TO BE A FILM STAR...
...JUST LIKE BRONCO BILLY ANDERSON.

THE MOMENT HE OPENS HIS MOUTH, NO ONE WOULD EVER MISTAKE BUBBA FOR A MONTANA COWHAND...
B-71
...BUT, OF COURSE, THE PICTURES ARE SILENT...
...AND IT'S THAT BEAUTIFULLY EXPRESSIVE FACE OF HIS THAT'S HIS CHARM.
...AND HOW DELICIOUS YOU'LL BE.
PLEASE-- WE'VE GOT TO GO--
--BUT THE SHIP -- IT'S SINKING --
WE'RE NOT GOING ANYWHERE, SWEET DARLING BOY.
OH, GOD.
NOT ONE GOD, BUT TWO...

THAT'S OF NO CONSEQUENCE TO YOU OR ME.
I'VE MADE A CHOICE...
...TO MAKE NO CHOICES...
...BUT INSTEAD TO LET FATE CHOOSE YOU FOR ME...
...AND TO HER CREDIT, FATE HAS SERVED ME WELL.
NO-- PLEASE.
MUCH MORE OF THAT, DARLING SWEET BOY...
...I LOVE IT WHEN YOU BEG.

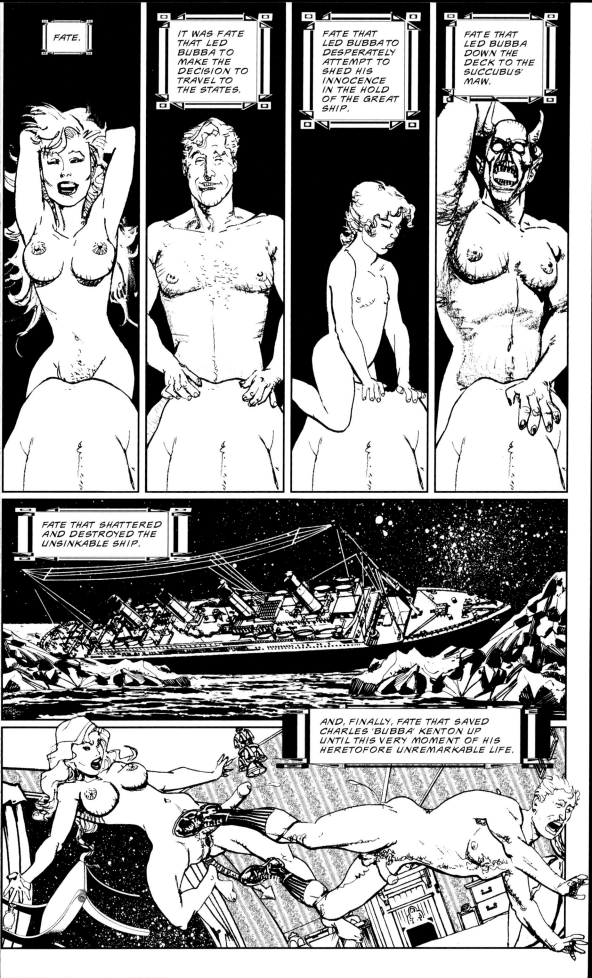

FATE.

IT WAS FATE THAT LED BUBBA TO MAKE THE DECISION TO TRAVEL TO THE STATES,

FATE THAT LED BUBBA TO DESPERATELY ATTEMPT TO SHED HIS INNOCENCE IN THE HOLD OF THE GREAT SHIP,

FATE THAT LED BUBBA DOWN THE DECK TO THE SUCCUBUS' MAW.

FATE THAT SHATTERED AND DESTROYED THE UNSINKABLE SHIP.

AND, FINALLY, FATE THAT SAVED CHARLES 'BUBBA' KENTON UP UNTIL THIS VERY MOMENT OF HIS HERETOFORE UNREMARKABLE LIFE.

YEARS FROM NOW, DRUNK ON THE BLOOD AND FLESH OF INNOCENTS, BUBBA WILL ENGAGE WITH THE CENTRAL TRUTH OF HIS EXISTENCE...
GUH, UH, HUH, HUH...
...THAT HE WAS RESCUED, SAVED FROM CERTAIN DEATH BY DROWNING..
...COURTESY OF ANAL RAPE BY A SEXUALLY INSATIABLE SUCCUBUS...
...A CARNAL DEMON WHO TOOK WHAT WAS LEFT OF HIS INNOCENCE...
...AND LEFT BEHIND THE FIERY POX THAT WOULD CONSUME ALL OF BUBBA'S HUMANITY...
...LEAVING HIM A HOST AND CARRIER FOR HIS/HER/ITS VILE AND UTTERLY DISGUSTING AND INSATIABLE DESIRE...
...WHICH SOUNDS A LOT LIKE HIS FIRST NIGHT BITING HIS PILLOW IN PUBLIC SCHOOL.

THERE ARE THOSE WHO LOOK UPON THE TITANIC DISASTER AS A METAPHOR...
...THAT THE LOSS OF THE SUPPOSEDLY UNSINKABLE SHIP SERVED AS A MORAL PRELUDE TO THE GREAT WAR...
...THAT HER BUILDERS' PRESUMPTIONS WERE THE FIRST BLOW IN AN ASSAULT ON NATURE...
...AN ATTACK THAT WOULD REACH ITS CULMINATION IN THE MECHANIZATION OF WARFARE IN THE TRENCHES OF FRANCE, BELGIUM AND FLANDERS...
...AS THE INDUSTRIAL AGE TRANSFORMED WAR BETWEEN NATIONS FROM AN OPPORTUNITY TO DIE IN GLORY...
...INTO A GRUESOME FACTORY OF FLESH, BLOOD AND BONE.
FLESH, BLOOD AND BONE.

I BEG YOUR PARDON...?
JUST THINKING OUT LOUD.
ABOUT THOSE POOR SOULS.
WHO...
...OH. YOU MEAN --
-- THE ONES WHO AREN'T US.
WE'LL JUST HAVE TO SEE ABOUT THAT...
YES. WE'RE THE LUCKY ONES.
...WON'T WE?
AND THE GOUT OF BLOOD GLISTENED IN THE FROZEN STARLIGHT.
END OF CHAPTER TWO.

HOLLYWOODLAND
HOLLYWOOD, CALIFORNIA...
...EARLY WINTER, 1919.
JUST ANOTHER SHITTY LITTLE OIL AND CATTLE TOWN...
...FOUNDED BY PIOUSLY HYPOCRITICAL MIDWESTERNERS...
...WHO BROUGHT THEIR PREJUDICES WITH THEM TO THE EDGE OF AMERICA.
THEY BUILT THE SAME HOUSES THAT SERVED THEM IN PEORIA, OSHKOSH AND OMAHA...
...IN A DESPERATE ATTEMPT TO BRING THE MIDWEST TO THE FAR WEST...
...AND THEN THE MOVIE PEOPLE CAME ALONG AND COMPLETELY FUCKED THINGS UP.
SLOW DOWN, YOU STUPID CUNT--
--AH--
--THAT'S MORE LIKE IT, EUNICE.
BE NICE, DEVORA--
GO FUCK YOURSELF, DEREK.
--I'M SIMPLY SAYING ONE NEVER KNOWS WHO ONE'S FUCKING...
...BUBBA THINKS THIS ONE MIGHT BE BIG.
OH, PLEASE--
--THE ONLY THING THAT POMMY PUSSY THINKS IS BIG HERE IS YOUR DICK.
AS ALWAYS, MY DEAR, YOU'RE TOO KIND...

....BUT IT IS TRUE THAT, EXCEPT FOR BUBBA, I'VE GOT THE BIGGEST COCK ON A WHITE MAN WEST OF THE ROCKIES.
THERE'S HARDLY ANY NEED TO GO AROUND BRAGGING ABOUT SUCH THINGS, DEREK, OLD BOY...
...IT FEELS SO TERRIBLY UNSEEMLY.
JUST HOLDING MY OWN.
AND WITH A WIFE LIKE YOURS, MR. BROADBENT, I'D BET YO DO A LOT OF HOLDING OF YOUR OWN.
DEVORA'S A RIGHT DAME...
CERTAINLY--
--IF YOUR DEFINITION OF 'RIGHT' IS PUSSY-LAPPING FIELD WHORE.
NOW, NOW, BUBBA--
--JUST BECAUSE SHE SAID NO TO YOU DOESN'T MEAN SHE'S A SAPPHIST.
IT'S BEEN SEVEN YEARS SINCE BUBBA'S LIFE WAS SAVED...
NO--
--THAT'S CONFIRMED BY HER OBSESSION WITH MY PROTEGE, EUNICE HERE.
I'D HARDLY CALL IT AN OBSESSION, MR. KENTON...
...DEVORA JUST KNOWS WHOSE FACE SERVES BEST AS A SEAT.

NOW KEEP IT CLEAN, BUBBA--
LIVE IN DREAMS, H.L.--
--I CAN FEEL THAT COCK OF HIS THROUGH THREE LAYERS OF CRINOLINE.
AND HERE I THOUGHT YOU'D BE FLATTERED...
...RESCUED FROM CERTAIN, WATERY DEATH BY A BRUTAL ANAL RAPE...
...AT THE HANDS AND DICK OF A SEXUALLY RAPACIOUS AND INSATIABLE HERMAPHRODITIC DEMON.
...SINCE EVERY RED-BLOODED AMERICAN BOY OUT THERE IN THE DARK WANTS TO SLIP YOU THE PORK, TOO.
I'VE NEVER BEEN SO INSULTED IN MY LIFE.
I'D SUGGEST YOU GET OUT MORE.
ARE YOU ALL RIGHT, MR. KENTON?
YES, OF COURSE, EUNICE MY DEAR--
--IT'S JUST THIS HEAT AND LIGHT WREAKS HAVOC WITH MY DELICATE CONDITION.
DELICATE CONDITION?
I'M TERRIBLY SENSITIVE TO THE SUN...
...WHICH MAKES WORKING IN THE MOVIE BUSINESS DICEY AT BEST...

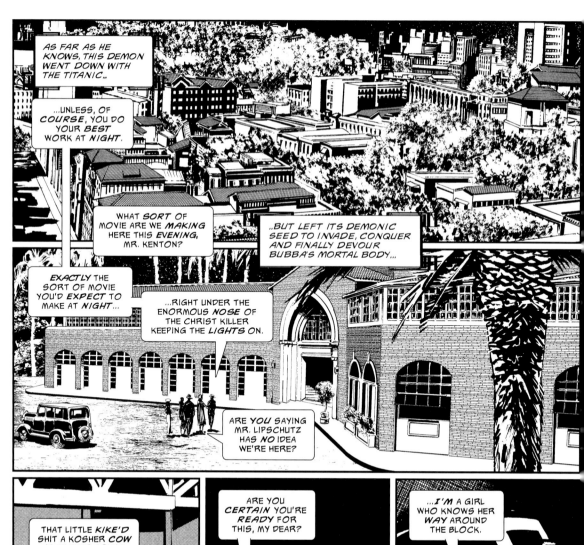

AS FAR AS HE KNOWS, THIS DEMON WENT DOWN WITH THE TITANIC...

...UNLESS, OF *COURSE*, YOU DO YOUR *BEST* WORK AT *NIGHT*.

WHAT *SORT* OF MOVIE ARE WE *MAKING* HERE THIS *EVENING*, MR. KENTON?

..BUT LEFT ITS DEMONIC SEED TO INVADE, CONQUER AND FINALLY DEVOUR BUBBA'S MORTAL BODY...

EXACTLY THE SORT OF MOVIE YOU'D *EXPECT* TO MAKE AT *NIGHT*...

...RIGHT UNDER THE ENORMOUS *NOSE* OF THE CHRIST KILLER KEEPING THE *LIGHTS* ON.

ARE *YOU* SAYING MR. LIPSCHUTZ HAS *NO* IDEA WE'RE HERE?

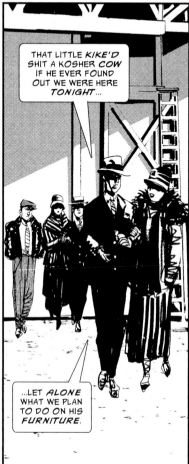

THAT LITTLE *KIKE'D* SHIT A KOSHER *COW* IF HE EVER FOUND OUT WE WERE HERE *TONIGHT*...

...LET *ALONE* WHAT WE PLAN TO DO ON HIS *FURNITURE*.

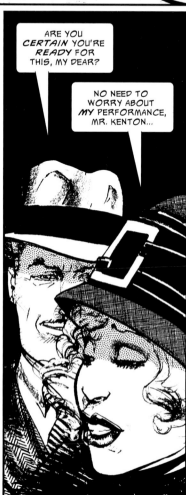

ARE YOU *CERTAIN* YOU'RE *READY* FOR THIS, MY DEAR?

NO NEED TO WORRY ABOUT *MY* PERFORMANCE, MR. KENTON...

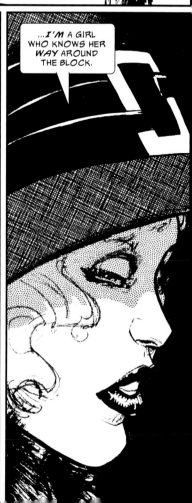

...*I'M* A GIRL WHO KNOWS HER *WAY* AROUND THE BLOCK.

NOW JUST RELAX, EUNICE...
...WE'RE JUST GOING TO DO WHAT COMES NATURALLY HERE.
FROM WHAT MISS HUNTLEY AND MR. BROADBENT HAVE SAID, I'M GUESSING I'M IN FOR A TREAT.
...TURNING HIM INTO A DEMON HIMSELF, CURSED, OR PERHAPS BLESSED, WITH THAT SAME INSATIABLE HUNGER...
THERE'S NO NEED FOR BULLSHIT, EUNICE--
--DEVORA DESPISES ME, AND DEREK WOULD LIKE NOTHING BETTER THAN MY MANMEAT SHOVED UP HIS ASS.
BUT I DO HAVE ONE ADVANTAGE OVER MY FELLOW MAN...
...A HUNGER FOR ALL THE SINS OF THE FLESH...
...WHEREAS MOST MEN ARE LIMITED BY THEIR FLESH...
...I AM GIFTED WITH THE ABILITY TO ACCOMMODATE ANY PUSSY OR ASSHOLE AROUND.

TAKE YOUR TIME, EUNICE...
...WE WANT TO MILK THE MOMENT.
NOW I WANT A LOOK OF WONDER, FEAR AND RESPECT--
IS THAT ALL?
THERE'S NO CALL FOR CLEVERNESS FROM YOU, YOUNG WOMAN...
ENOUGH WONDER, FEAR AND RESPECT FOR YOU, MR. KENTON?
SINCE YOU'LL BE SUCKING MY DICK, WE CAN DROP THE FORMALITY...
...CALL ME BUBBA.
IT'S AWFULLY BIG.
NO SHIT...
...AND IT GETS BIGGER.

AND IT WILL KEEP GETTING BIGGER UNTIL IT EXPLODES FROM INSIDE YOU...
OH-- MY GOD!
...UNTIL YOU PLEDGE YOUR LIFE, YOUR WILL AND YOUR FUTURE TO ME AND MY MASTER.
YOU--
YOU'RE MY MAS--
--GUHHUUCKK!
I AM BUT A SERVANT...
...AND ONCE YOU'VE SWALLOWED MY LOVE, YOU'LL SERVE MY MASTER, TOO.
...AND A HUNGER FOR THE FLESH AND BLOOD ITSELF.
A DEMON.

A VAMPIRE,
A SUCCUBUS,
MERE WORDS...
...BARELY DEFINITIONS...
...AND HONESTLY, WHEN ALL IS SAID AND DONE...
...WHO TRULY GIVES A SHIT WHAT THEY'RE CALLED?

WHAT HAVE YOU DONE TO ME, YOU FUCKING BASTARD?
THEY SERVE THAT TWO-FACED GOD...
I CAN ONLY HOPE, MY DEAR, THAT I'VE MADE MYSELF A PARTNER...
...SOMEONE WITH WHOM I CAN SHARE THIS EXTRAORDINARY LIFE OF MINE.
SEE?
I TOLD YOU HE HAD NO INTENTION OF--
SHUT UP, DEVORA.
YES...

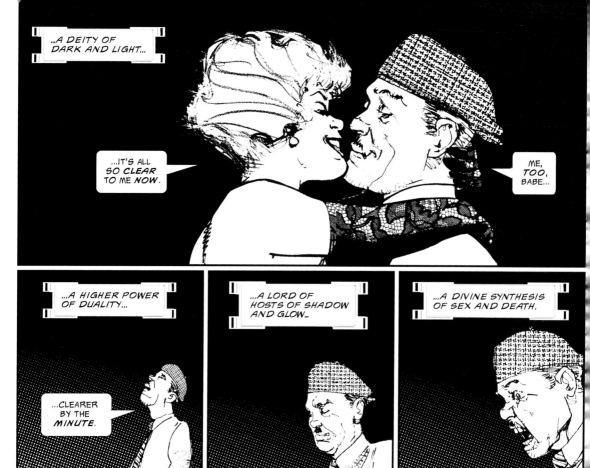

...A DEITY OF DARK AND LIGHT...

...IT'S ALL SO CLEAR TO ME NOW.

ME, TOO, BABE...

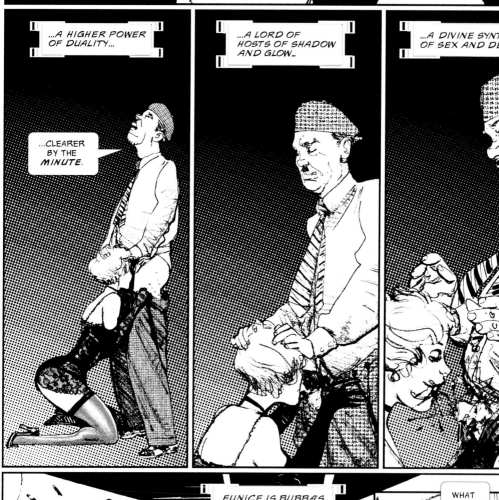

...A HIGHER POWER OF DUALITY...

...A LORD OF HOSTS OF SHADOW AND GLOW...

...CLEARER BY THE MINUTE.

...A DIVINE SYNTHESIS OF SEX AND DEATH.

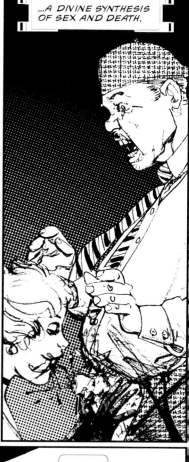

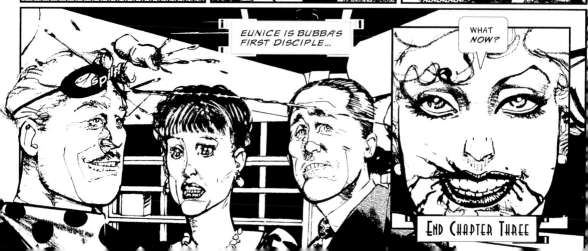

EUNICE IS BUBBA'S FIRST DISCIPLE...

WHAT NOW?

END CHAPTER THREE

CHRISTMAS EVE, 1931.
MEXICO...
...ZONA NORTE, TIJUANA.
HEY, HEY HEY--!
--CALL ME CRAZY...
...BUT THAT'S GOTTA HURT, EVEN GOIN' IN FROM THE FRONT AND THE TOP, DON'TCHA THINK?
YOU OUGHT TO KNOW, BUBBA, DARLING...
...THAT DICK LOOKS TO BE ABOUT THE SAME SIZE AS THAT IRON JOHN I HAD UP YOUR ASS LAST NIGHT.
JEALOUS, DEREK?
DON'T START, DEVORA.
ALWAYS TELLING TALES OUT OF SCHOOL, AREN'T WE, EUNICE?
I MAY BE THE MOTHER OF YOUR CHILD, BUBBA, BUT IF YOU CALL ME THAT AGAIN I'LL CUT YOUR DICK OFF AND MAKE YOU EAT IT--
--IT'S ILONA FONTAINE, AND DON'T YOU FORGET IT.

BACK IN THIS EARLY HEYDAY OF CROSS-BORDER AND CROSS-CULTURAL DECADENCE...
...EL ZONA NORTE WAS THE PLACE TO BE FOR MORAL DECAY AT ITS FINEST...
...AND THE HOTEL AGUA CALIENTE WAS THE ABSOLUTE PINNACLE...
...OR, PERHAPS, THE VERY NADIR...
...OF THOSE UNEARTHLY DELIGHTS...
...AND NOTHING SAID DEGENERACY BACK IN THOSE EARLY DEPRESSION DAYS...
...WITH QUITE THE SAME COURAGE OF ITS CONVICTIONS...
...AS THE PANSY CRAZE SWEEPING THE BACK ALLEYS OF BOTH NATIONS...
...CELEBRATED BY A BLACK AND WHITE DRAG BALL.
NO NEED TO BE SUCH A CUNT, ILONA...
WHAT DO YOU SAY YOU LEAVE THAT DECISION TO ME, EH, BUBBA?
I HATE IT WHEN THEY FIGHT LIKE THIS, DON'T YOU?
FRANKLY, DEREK, THE ONLY REASON I PUT UP WITH ANY OF THIS SHIT...
...IS MY SOLEMN PRAYER THAT ONE OF THEM WILL QUIT FUCKING ABOUT AND MAKE ME IMMORTAL.

FUCK ME, DEVORA, BUT DO YOU SEE THAT?
I DO, I DO--
--BETCHA I KNOW WHO HIS FAVORITE MOVIE STAR IS, HUH, HONEY?
WHO THE FUCK'RE YOU S'POSED TO BE, MISS THING?
THE REAL THING, YOU LITTLE QUEER.
I BLEED AND BREED--
OH, GOD--
--MORE THAN I CAN SAY FOR YOU, I'LL BET.
I'M SO SORRY, MISS FONTAINE...
...YOU'RE MY FAVORITE FILM STAR, TRULY YOU ARE.
I'M TERRIBLY FLATTERED, MR.--
LAINE-- MISS DAGMAR LAINE.
WELL, ILONA DARLING, YOU MAY BE FLATTERED, BUT THIS OLD BOY IS AS HARD AS A ROCK AT HOW INTERESTING THIS EVENING JUST GOT TO BE...
...QUESTION IS...
...WHICH TWIN GETS TO RIDE THE BIGGEST DICK IN HOLLYWOOD FIRST?

Y'KNOW, WITH THE TALKING PICTURES HERE TO STAY...
...NOBODY BELIEVES ME AS THE ONLY LAW WEST OF THE PECOS THE MINUTE I OPEN MY MOUTH...
...AND IT'S NOT MONTANA OR WYOMING COMES OUT, BUT THE COTSWOLDS...
...SO MAYBE I'LL BECOME A DIRECTOR...
WAIT'LL THE OTHER GIRLS HEAR ABOUT THIS.
FUCK THAT, FAGGOT--
--YOU BREATHE A WORD OF THIS TO ANYONE, YOU'LL END UP ON BOTH SIDES OF THE TROLLEY TRACKS.
NOT TO WORRY, SWEETIE--
--IF THAT DICK O' YOURS IS AS BIG AS THEY SAY, MY VOCAL CORDS AIN'T GONNA BE WORTH SHIT, NO HOW.
...'CAUSE SURE AS SHIT GOTTA BE SOMEBODY'D PAY BIG MONEY TO SEE THIS, DON'TCHA KNOW?
CHRIST ON CRUTCHES--

--SO I GUESS OLYMPUS THE WONDER HORSE DIES OF JEALOUSY EVERY TIME YOU TAKE A PISS.
YOU DO GO ON--
LAST TIME I HAD SOMETHING THAT BIG UP MY ASS, I COULDN'T SIT DOWN FOR A WEEK.
THAT'S ENOUGH, DAGMAR--
HE'S A BIG ENOUGH ASSHOLE AS IT IS WITHOUT THE FLATTERY.
DON'T LISTEN TO HER, YOU SWEET LITTLE SISSY...
...WE BOTH KNOW YOU'VE BEEN THINKING ABOUT NOTHING BUT MY BALLS ON YOUR CHIN SINCE WE MET.
DO YOU REALLY BELIEVE YOUR OWN BULLSHIT, BUBBA?
I DON'T HAVE TO, ILONA--
--IT'S HARDLY A SECRET THAT EVERY PANSY IN THE WORLD IS RAVENOUSLY HUNGRY FOR DICK...

...AND WHEN IT'S MY DICK WE'RE TALKING ABOUT...
...AND THE QUEER IN QUESTION WANTS NOTHING MORE THAN TO BE FUCKED BY ME WHILE HE'S DOLLED UP TO LOOK LIKE YOU...
...I'D CALL THAT KISMET, DON'TCHA KNOW?
OH MY GOD!
I--
--REST--
--MY CASE!
IT'S BEEN LIKE THIS SINCE THE DAY THEY MET...
...AND ILONA, NEE EUNICE MacAVOY, FEARS IT'S ALWAYS GOING TO BE THIS WAY...
...AND WHEN YOU'RE LOOKING AT A FUNCTION-ALLY STERILE LIFE AS A BLOODSUCKING, FLESH-EATING SUCCUBUS...

...ALWAYS CAN BE A REAL PROBLEM...
YOU DO LOVE IT, DON'T YOU?
YOU KNOW I DO, DADDY...
...WHY ARE YOU STOPPING?
IT'S TIME FOR YOU BOTH TO DO A LITTLE LIGHT HOUSEKEEPING...
...IT JUST WON'T DO FOR MY MAN MEAT TO BE SMEARED WITH SOME FAGGOT'S SHIT...
...SO LET'S GET CLEANED UP, SHALL WE?
WHEN SHE WAS STILL EUNICE MacAVOY, SHE HAD PLANS, BIG PLANS, FOR A FUTURE IN THE SHOW BUSINESS.
UNTIL THIS MOMENT, ILONA HAS BEEN SIMPLY ADRIFT IN HER LIFE.

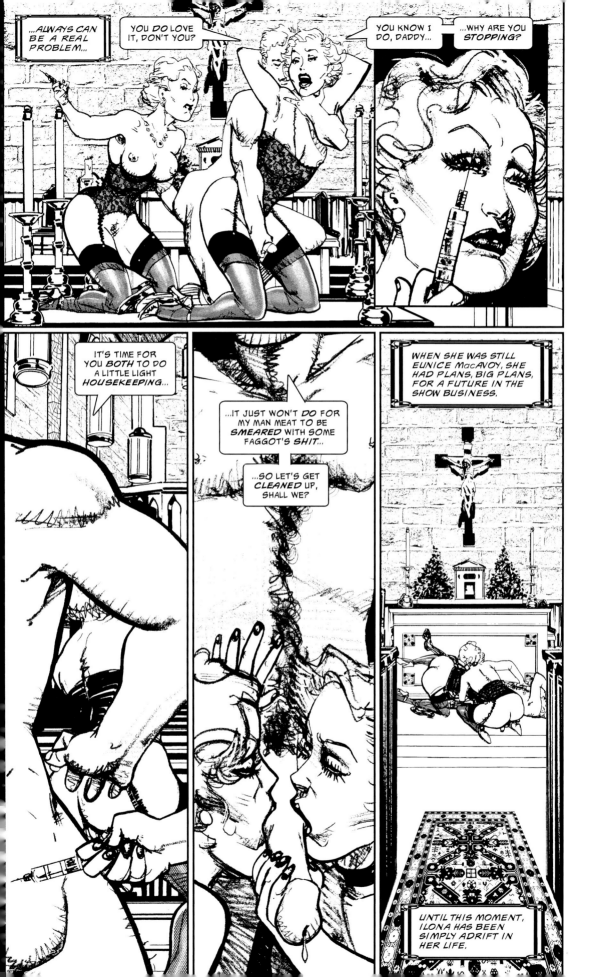

FROM THE MOMENT SHE WAS TRANSFORMED BY BUBBA'S DEMONIC JISM, SHE'S BEEN HIS CONSTANT COMPANION.

UNTIL THIS MOMENT, SHE NEVER KNEW THERE WAS SOMETHING ELSE SHE MIGHT HAVE WANTED.

THANKS TO HER CONNECTIONS WITH BUBBA, SHE DRIFTED INTO A MEANINGLESS CAREER OF SECOND-TIER ROLES IN THIRD-RATE MOVIES.

UNTIL THIS MOMENT, SHE NEVER KNEW THERE WERE OTHER POSSIBILITIES AVAILABLE TO HER.

WITH THE ARRIVAL OF SOUND, BUBBA'S RIDICULOUS CAREER AS A COWBOY HAD COME TO AN ABRUPT AND UNEXPECTED END.

UNTIL THIS MOMENT, SHE HAD NO IDEA SHE MIGHT SEPARATE HERSELF FROM THE MONSTER HE'D BECOME.

WITH PROFESSIONAL PROSPECTS GROWING DIMMER BY THE DAY, ILONA, FRIENDLESS AT BEST, HAS HAD NO ONE TO GUIDE HER DECISIONS.

UNTIL THIS DAY, SHE HAD NEVER CONSIDERED ANY OTHER ROAD THAN THE ONE THAT SEEMED ORDAINED BY THAT HERMAPHRODITIC GOD.

TELEGRAM FOR SENOR BROADBENT--
--SENOR BROADBENT...
OVER HERE, BOY...
...AND DO STOP SHOUTING, POR FAVOR.
WHAT IS IT, DEREK?
HOLD YOUR WATER, DEVOR--
--HOLY SHIT.
HOLY SHIT, INDEED.
THAT CUNT...

"...THAT FUCKING CUNT."
YOU SURE WE DID THE RIGHT THING BACK THERE, MISS FONTAINE?
IF I'D KNOWN THEN WHAT I KNOW NOW...
...I WOULD'VE FUCKED HIS HORSE.
AND SPEAKING OF FUCKING...
IF IT'S GOING TO BE YOU AND ME FOR THE WHILE, IT'S TIME YOU STARTED CALLING ME ILONA.
YES, M--
--ILONA.
HAPPY?
YER KIDDIN', RIGHT?
I'M THE HAPPIEST GIRL IN THE WORLD.
END CHAPTER FOUR

Spring. 1942... ...Occupied Paris...

...the 18th Arrondissement. Montmartre.

NEARLY TWO YEARS OF GERMAN OCCUPATION HAS TURNED WHAT WAS ONCE UNTHINKABLE INTO THE NORM...

...PARISIANS AND THEIR INVADERS LEARN TO GET ALONG TO GET ALONG...

...WITH NEITHER SIDE TRULY CONSIDERING THE CONSEQUENCES OF WHATEVER OUTCOME THE STILL-RAGING WAR WILL BRING.

BUT, PARIS BEING PARIS, LIFE GOES ON...

...AND, OF COURSE, PARIS BEING PARIS, LIFE MEANS NIGHTLIFE...

...SO, WHILE THE AVERAGE PARISIAN GREETS LES BOCHES WITH SMILES THAT MIGHT OCCASIONALLY BARELY MASK CONTEMPT...

...THE ONE-TIME CITY OF LIGHTS OPENS ITS ARMS TO ANYONE WITH THE FRANCS TO PAY FOR A GOOD TIME.

THE TENNESSEE STUD WAS LONG AND LEAN...

...THE COLOR OF THE SUN AND HIS EYES WERE GREEN...

...HE HAD THE NERVE...

...AND HE HAD THE BLOOD...

...THERE NEVER WAS A MAN LIKE THE TENNESSEE STUD.

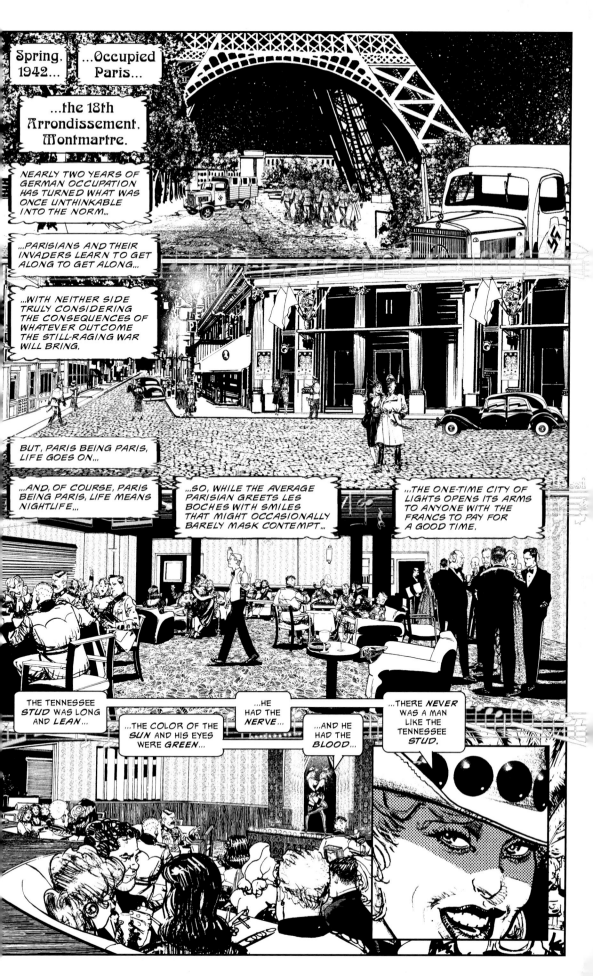

SOMEWHERE, SOMETIME IN THE LAST DECADE, ILONA FONTAINE FADED INTO FORGOTTEN, DUSTY NOTHINGNESS...
...HER PLACE TAKEN BY BLANCHE DeWOLFE.
PRESENT COMPANY EXCEPTED, OF COURSE -- RIGHT, STANDARTENFÜHRER, HONEY?
I NEVER ARGUE WITH A WOMAN.
OH, I DON'T KNOW...
...YOUR DATE THERE LOOKS LIKE SHE'S SPOILIN' FOR A FIGHT.
NOW, NOW, DAGMAR...
...THERE'S ENOUGH SORROW IN THE WORLD AS IT IS...
QUITE RIGHT...
...THERE'S NO GOOD REASON TO START ANY MORE TROUBLE.
AND SOMEWHERE IN THAT DECADE, BLANCHE AND DAGMAR, HER DEVOTED THRALL, ENDED UP IN THE CITY OF LIGHT.
ALTHOUGH I HAVE TO SAY MY SISTER HAS A POINT...
...THAT WHORE YOU'RE FUCKING HAS A MOUTH LIKE A CHICKEN'S ASSHOLE...
...AND HERE I THOUGHT IT WAS THE FRENCH...

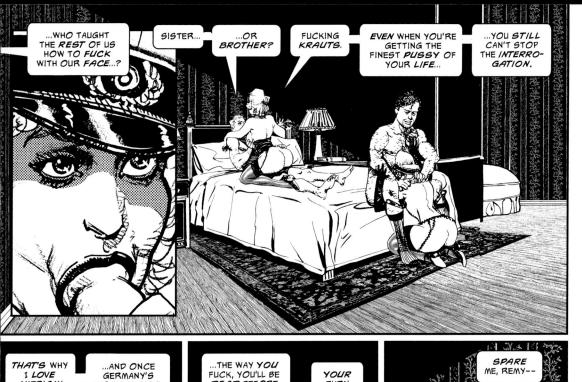

...WHO TAUGHT THE *REST* OF US HOW TO *FUCK* WITH OUR *FACE*...?

SISTER...

...OR *BROTHER*?

FUCKING KRAUTS.

EVEN WHEN YOU'RE GETTING THE FINEST *PUSSY* OF YOUR *LIFE*...

...YOU *STILL* CAN'T STOP THE *INTERROGATION*.

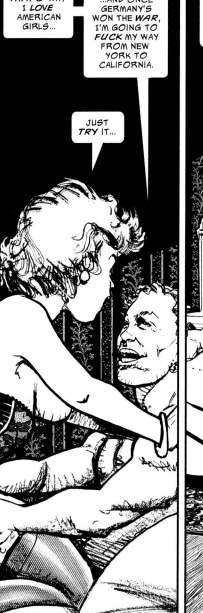

THAT'S WHY I *LOVE* AMERICAN GIRLS...

...AND ONCE GERMANY'S WON THE *WAR*, I'M GOING TO *FUCK* MY WAY FROM NEW YORK TO CALIFORNIA.

JUST *TRY* IT...

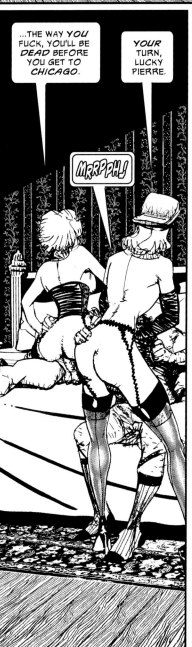

...THE WAY *YOU* FUCK, YOU'LL BE *DEAD* BEFORE YOU GET TO *CHICAGO*.

YOUR TURN, LUCKY PIERRE.

MRRRPH!

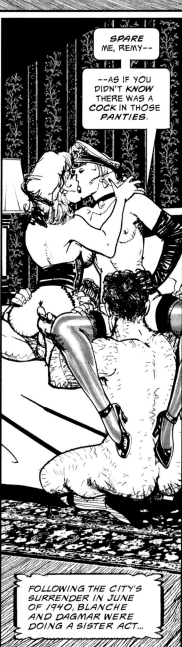

SPARE ME, REMY--

--AS IF YOU DIDN'T *KNOW* THERE WAS A *COCK* IN THOSE *PANTIES*.

FOLLOWING THE CITY'S SURRENDER IN JUNE OF 1940, BLANCHE AND DAGMAR WERE DOING A SISTER ACT...

...AND RATHER THAN TAKE THEIR CHANCES AND TRY TO MAKE IT TO THE SWISS BORDER...
Mmm?
NOT QUITE YET, SWEET...
...BLANCHE AND DAGMAR OPTED TO RIDE OUT THE WAR IN PARIS...
...BECAUSE WHILE THE REST OF THE COUNTRY WAS SUBSISTING ON SCRAPS FROM THE INVADER'S TABLE...
...ENTERTAINERS IN GENERAL, AND GORGEOUS, ENGAGING AND PROFOUNDLY FUCKABLE BLONDE ENTERTAINERS IN PARTICULAR...
...WERE ABLE TO SURVIVE, AND EVEN THRIVE, UNDER THE RELENTLESS ASS-FUCKING THE FRENCH GOT FROM THEIR LONGSTANDING ENEMY...
...AN ENEMY ALL TOO READY TO PAY THE FRENCH BACK FOR THE ANAL RAPE THEY GOT IN THE COMPIÉGNE FOREST BACK IN 1918.
NOW?

NOW.
OH, GOD--
--I'M CUMMING!!
THEY'VE DONE THIS BEFORE...
...FUCKING, THEN SLAUGHTERING, GERMAN OFFICERS...
CHUNDIT!
...AND COLLABORATORS ALIKE.
NOT OUT OF PATRIOTISM, OR PARTISANSHIP...
I'LL ALMOST MISS REMY, HERE--
KYUNSCCH!
...OR EVEN A SENSE OF JUSTICE.
SIMPLY PUT, BLANCHE AND DAGMAR ARE ROMANTICS...
--IT ISN'T EVERY DAY YOU FIND A STRAIGHT MAN WHO KNOWS HIS WAY AROUND A COCK.
...AND THE BRUTAL MURDERS OF GERMAN OFFICERS AND COLLABORATORS ARE ALL ABOUT LOVE.
GEORGES--!
DAMN IT, DAGMAR--
--WHERE THE FUCK IS YOUR BOYFRIEND WITH THE GETAWAY CAR?

THAT MUST BE HIM...
LIKE HELL IT IS.
RUN, AND WE'LL RENDEZVOUS AT THE USUAL PLACE.
BUT, GEORGES—
FUCK GEORGES...
...BECAUSE HE SURE AS SHIT FUCKED US, BUT GOOD.
RELAX, MEIN SCHEINE SCHWANZLUTSCHER...
...WE'RE ALL GOOD FRIENDS HERE.
UNNGGH!
WHY WASTE A PUNCH ON HER STOMACH, WERNER--
--GO RIGHT FOR THE BALLS, FOR FUCK'S SAKE.
UNNCCCHH

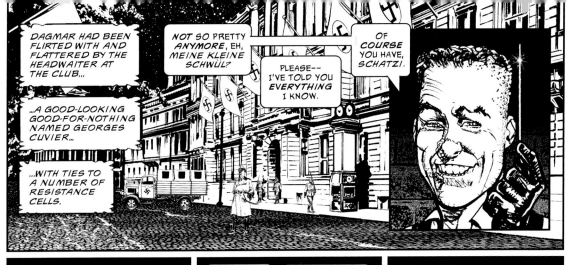

DAGMAR HAD BEEN FLIRTED WITH AND FLATTERED BY THE HEADWAITER AT THE CLUB...

...A GOOD-LOOKING GOOD-FOR-NOTHING NAMED GEORGES CUVIER...

...WITH TIES TO A NUMBER OF RESISTANCE CELLS.

NOT SO PRETTY ANYMORE, EH, MEINE KLEINE SCHWÜL?

PLEASE-- I'VE TOLD YOU EVERYTHING I KNOW.

OF COURSE YOU HAVE, SCHATZI.

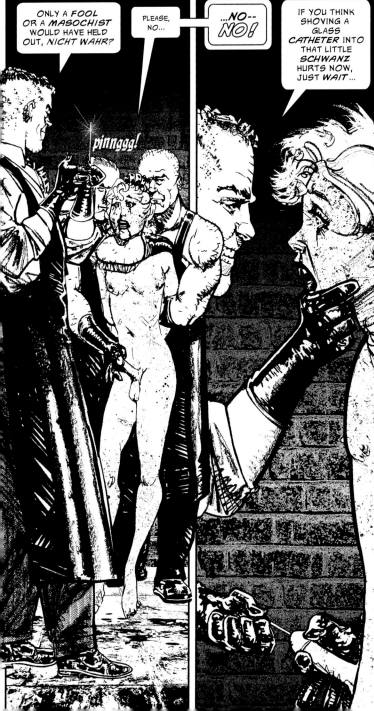

ONLY A FOOL OR A MASOCHIST WOULD HAVE HELD OUT, NICHT WAHR?

PLEASE, NO...

...NO-- NO!

IF YOU THINK SHOVING A GLASS CATHETER INTO THAT LITTLE SCHWANZ HURTS NOW, JUST WAIT...

pinnggg!

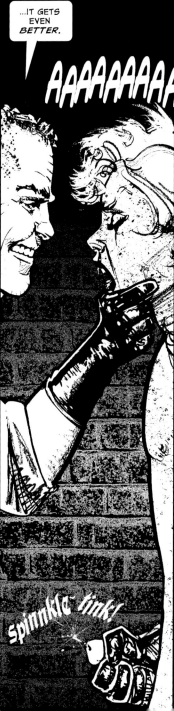

...IT GETS EVEN BETTER.

AAAAAAAAA

spinnkle tink!

AAAAAAAAAAAAAAAAAAAAAAAAAAAAAAAAAAAAAAAAA
DID YOU GET ANYTHING FROM HER?
NOTHING WE DIDN'T KNOW ALREADY, THANKS TO YOU.
SORRY THE OTHER ONE GOT AWAY, THOUGH.
OH, WE'LL GET HER..
...AND, OF COURSE, IF THERE'S ANYTHING YOU CAN DO TO HELP...
AAAAAAAAAAAAAAAAAAAAAAAAAAAAAAAAAAAAAAAAA
I'LL KEEP MY EYES AND EARS OPEN, HAUPTSTURMFÜHRER RAHN...
...AND, OF COURSE, CONVEY MY BEST WISHES TO STURMBAHNFÜHRER ALTBUSSER.
AAAAAAAAAAAAAAAAAAAAAAAAAAAAAAAAAAAAAAAAA
VROOOOOOMM!

I HAVE TO SAY I'M SURPRISED...
...I WAS SURE THE STURMBAHNFÜHRER WOULD WANT TO WITNESS THIS.
YEAH--BUT HIS WIFE CALLED, AND...
...WE BOTH KNOW HOW THAT GOES.
IT'S A JOB THAT CAN BE TOUGH ON YOUR HOME LIFE.
HOW VERY, VERY TRUE.
IF MY MRS. KNEW HALF OF WHAT WE GO THROUGH HERE, HER HAIR WOULD STAND ON END.
klik
AND THAT'S WHY MY ALPHONSINE AND I HAVE AN AGREEMENT...
...SHE DOESN'T FILL ME IN ON WHAT HAPPENS AT HER KAFFEE KLATSCH...
shik
...AND I KEEP MUM ABOUT MY WORK DAY.
WORKS FOR ME, TOO.
Chunggkkk-THUDD.

I HOPED I'D FIND YOU HERE.
Y'KNOW, I'M OLDER THAN I LOOK, GEORGES...
...A LOT OLDER...
...AND I SPENT AN AWFULLY LONG TIME LOOKING FOR SOMEONE EXACTLY LIKE DAGMAR.
NOW, THANKS TO YOU, I'VE LOST HER...
...AND I HAVE TO START ALL OVER AGAIN...
...WHICH IS MORE THAN I CAN SAY YOU'LL EVER HAVE THE CHANCE TO DO, YOU LYING SACK OF FRENCH SHIT.
JUST TWO ROMANTICS...
...ALL ABOUT THE LOVE.
End Chapter Five.

Summer, 1957...

...Orange County, California...

...Vanaheim.

ACCORDING TO THE LAST U.S. CENSUS, THE FASTEST-GROWING METROPOLITAN AREA IN THE UNITED STATES IS ORANGE COUNTY, CALIFORNIA...

...AND THE FASTEST-GROWING TOWN IN THE COUNTY IS VANAHEIM...

...A TOWN PREVIOUSLY BEST KNOWN AS THE BLOW JOB CAPITAL OF THE SOUTH BAY, WHERE BOYS FROM LOS ANGELES WENT TO POP THEIR CHERRIES.

THESE DAYS, SINCE KELTON MOSBY OPENED MOSBYLAND, HIS TRIBUTE TO HIS SCREENED MEMORY OF HIS OWN CHILDHOOD...

...THE HOOKERS, MOSTLY MEXICAN, WITH A FEW COLORED, AND MOSTLY WOMEN...

...HAVE HAD TO MOVE THEIR TRADE SOUTH TO OCEANSIDE, SAN DIEGO, AND ENCINITAS.

THE HOT SHEET MOTELS HAVE ALL GOTTEN A NEW COAT OF PAINT...

...A NUMBER OF THEM FREELY ADOPTING THE PROMISE OF THE WESTERN AMERICA THEME MOSBY'S MADE FAMOUS, AND THAT MADE HIM RICH ENOUGH...

...TO RISK HIS FORTUNE ON AN AMUSEMENT PARK WITHOUT THE USUAL GRINDHOUSE SLEAZINESS.

WHY DON'T YOU LET ME SUCK YOUR COCK, HONEY...

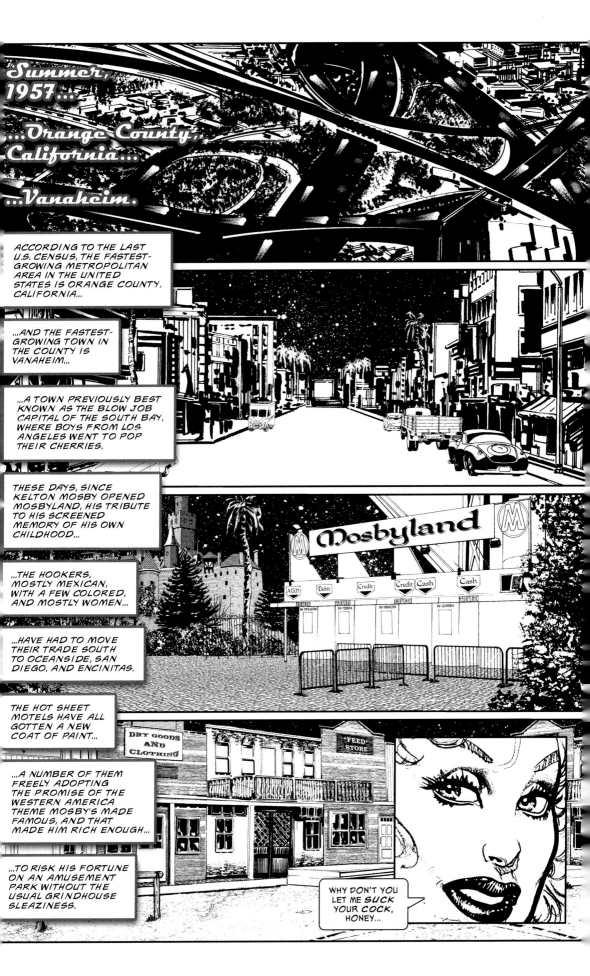

BUTCH CASSIDY
THE 'WILD BUNCH'
REWARD OF $2500
$500 Each
DEAD OR ALIVE!
BILLY THE KID
THE NOTORIOUS MONTANA MOUNTAIN MAN
$50,000
...CAUSE THERE SURE ISN'T ENOUGH THERE TO FILL MY PUSSY.
BEVERLY GROVE, a.k.a. BLANCHE DeWOLFE, a.k.a. ILONA FONTAINE, nee EUNICE MacAVOY, GREW UP IN A SMALL TOWN IN THE MIDWEST...
WHO THE FUCK YOU THINK YOU'RE TALKING TO, CUNT?
...SO THESE SURROUNDINGS...
REWARD
$10,000
DEAD OR ALIVE
YOU CAN STAND THERE WITH THAT LITTLE PEANUT IN YOUR HAND AND WHINE, YOUR FEELINGS ALL HURT...
...OR RATHER, THE RAW, UNIDEALIZED REALITY OF RURAL WESTERN AMERICAN LIFE AT THE DAWN OF THE 20th CENTURY...
$6,500 REWARD
...OR YOU CAN SHUT THE FUCK UP ABOUT IT AND LET ME GIVE YOU THE BLOW JOB OF A LIFETIME.
...IS ALL TOO MUCH A PART OF HER OWN PERSONAL MEMORY.
COCKSUCKER MOTHERFUCKER TWO-BALL BITCH!
THE SUNDANCE KID

OF COURSE, NONE OF THIS FANTASY REALLY CAPTURES THE TRUTH OF THAT TIME AND PLACE...
UNNNHHH...
...THE SMELL, THE SOUND, THE ATMOSPHERE...
...AAGGGGHHHH!!
...AND, OF COURSE, BEING HELD DOWN BY YOUR COUSINS SO THEY CAN GANG RAPE YOU FOR DECORATION DAY FOR THE PRICE OF YOUR FATHER'S CORN LIQUOR.
SO IT ISN'T THE RECREATION OF HER ALL-AMERICAN GIRLHOOD THAT DREW THE FORMER EUNICE MacAVOY TO MOSBYLAND...
GKKK...
SLASH
WHAT THE FUCK!!?!?
NEXT?

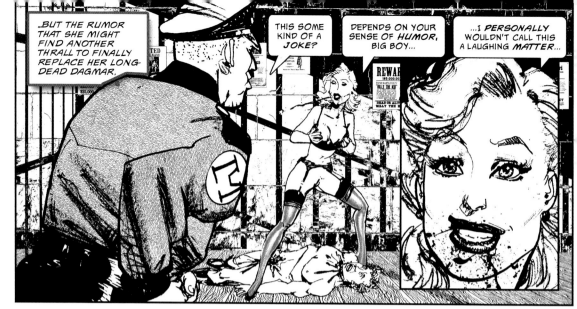

...BUT THE RUMOR THAT SHE MIGHT FIND ANOTHER THRALL TO FINALLY REPLACE HER LONG-DEAD DAGMAR.

THIS SOME KIND OF A JOKE?

DEPENDS ON YOUR SENSE OF *HUMOR*, BIG BOY...

...I *PERSONALLY* WOULDN'T CALL THIS A LAUGHING *MATTER*...

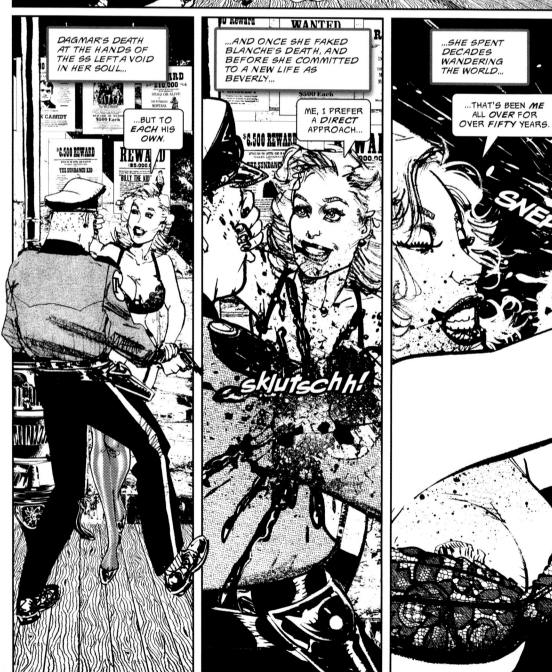

DAGMAR'S DEATH AT THE HANDS OF THE SS LEFT A VOID IN HER SOUL...

...BUT TO *EACH* HIS OWN.

...AND ONCE SHE FAKED BLANCHE'S DEATH, AND BEFORE SHE COMMITTED TO A NEW LIFE AS BEVERLY...

ME, I PREFER A *DIRECT* APPROACH...

sklutschh!

...SHE SPENT DECADES WANDERING THE WORLD...

...THAT'S BEEN *ME* ALL *OVER* FOR OVER *FIFTY* YEARS.

SNEPP

...LEAVING A STRING OF UNSOLVED GRISLY MURDERS IN HER WAKE.
WHAT'D I TELL YOU, RIGHT?
TOMORROW DINER
CAN THIS BABE SUCK COCK LIKE A FRENCH WHORE, OR WHAT?
NO SHIT.
WHERE'D YOU FIND HER, BOB?
SHE FOUND ME.
YEAH, RIGHT.
IT'S TRUE. SHE HEARD THAT, UNLIKE YOU, I REALLY AM HUNG LIKE A HORSE...
...AND SHE JUST HAD TO FIND OUT FOR HERSELF.
DIG THAT--
mmpphh!
--SEES A COLORED MAN, AND ALL SHE REALLY WANTS NOW IS TO SWALLOW A REAL DICK.
Y'ASK ME, LOOKS MORE LIKE THE LAST THING SHE WANTS IS NIGGER COCK.
WATCH THAT NIG--

HOLY SHIT...
...CHICK'S GOT A DICK!
PLEASE...
...PLEASE DON'T HIT ME...
...I'LL DO ANYTHING YOU WANT.
I SWEAR I WON'T TELL ANYONE.
WHATTAYA THINK?
Y'ASK ME, WE'RE HERE...
...SO WHY WASTE AN OPPORTUNITY LIKE THIS?
NO SHIT-- BE A STORY FOR THE GRANDCHILDREN.
MMPPFF!

IS IT JUST ME, OR WOULDN'T YOU THINK THIS FAGGOT WANTS TO BE A GIRL SO BAD...
MMMPPFFF!
...HE'D GO TO SWITZERLAND OR DENMARK OR WHEREVER TO GET THAT LITTLE COCK LOPPED.
NAH, NAH, NAH--
--THIS FAGGOT'S HARD AS A ROCK--
--AND NOW IT'S TIME TO SEE HOW HE LIKES DICK UP HIS ASS.
Butter
NO, PLEASE--
--I'M A VIRGIN!
NOT FOR LONG.
AND HEY, WHAT RED-BLOODED AMERICAN BOY DOESN'T WANT TO LOSE HIS VIRGINITY, RIGHT?
YOU KILL ME, BOB--JUST FUCKING KILL ME.

HEY--!
YOU EVEN THINK ABOUT BITING ME AGAIN, FAGGOT, AND I'LL CUT YOUR FUCKING THROAT--
--WE CLEAR ON THAT, YOU FUCKING SISSY?
I SAID, 'WE CLEAR?'
Mmm-mmm...
THAT'S BETTER, CANDYASS.
NOW MY FRIEND HERE'S JERKING HIS OWN DICK, FOR CHRIST'S SAKE--
--THE FUCK YOU GOOD FOR?
FUCK STEVE...
STEVE IS GONNA BE SO PISSED WE DIDN'T INVITE HIM.
...ANYWAY, HE CAN FUCK THIS FAGGOT'S ASS AFTER WE KILL HER.
RIGHT--SHE'LL STILL BE WARM ENOUGH FOR HIS DICK.
Tsk,tsk...
STEVE...?

NO...
...AND I'M WILLING TO BET *STEVE'S* GOING TO BE *FOREVER* GRATEFUL...
..TO HAVE BEEN LEFT *OUT* OF THIS LITTLE *MENAGE* OF YOURS.
FUCK ME *SIDEWAYS*, BUT HAVE I *DIED* AND GONE TO *HEAVEN?*
LOOKS LIKE THAT TO *ME*.
WHEN I WENT TO VORK FOR *MOSBY*, I TOOK HIM FOR A STICK-UP-HIS-ASS *SHITWIPE*...
...WHO KNEW *NIGHT LIFE* AT MOSBYLAND COULD BE SO MUCH *FUN?*
MOSBY'S ARCHITECTS MADE CERTAIN THAT ALL THE STRUCTURES WERE SOUNDPROOFED...
...TO CREATE, WHAT THE QUACK PSYCHIATRISTS HE HIRED AS CONSULTANTS REFERRED TO AS 'DISTINCT INTERIOR ENTERTAINMENT EXPERIENCES...'
TOMORROW DINER
OPEN
MONDAY THRU FRIDAY
7:00 AM TO 9:00 PM
SATURDAY AND SUNDAY
8:00 AM TO 6:00 PM
THE FOOD OF TOMORROW, TODAY!
TOMORROW DINER
...AN UNINTENDED CONSEQUENCE OF THIS WAS THAT THE SCREAMS WENT UNHEARD, AND THE BODIES WEREN'T DISCOVERED UNTIL OPENING TIME THE NEXT DAY.

WHAT WITH THE MILLIONS THAT HIS SO-CALLED 'FAMILY THEME PARK' BROUGHT TO VANAHEIM...
...MOSBY'S JUICE WITH THE LOCAL LAW AND PRESS WAS ENOUGH TO KEEP THE GRISLY DETAILS OF THE NIGHT'S EVENTS BURIED WELL BELOW THE PUBLIC RADAR.
ATM
Debit
Credit
Cash
Cash
NO SMOKING
NO ALCOHOL
VRRROOOOOOOMMM
WHO-- WHO-- ?
YOU CAN START WITH 'THANK YOU.'
THANKS, SURE--
--BUT HOW DID YOU DO THAT?
NOT IMPORTANT RIGHT NOW.
WHAT MATTERS IS THAT YOU'RE SAFE--
--AND WE'RE TOGETHER.
BUT--
TRUST ME--
--I'VE BEEN LOOKING FOR SOMEONE LIKE YOU FOR AN AWFULLY LONG TIME, DAGMAR.
YOU'VE GOT ME CONFUSED WITH SOMEBODY ELSE...
...MY NAME'S KIM.
NOT ANYMORE, DAGMAR, HONEY...
...NOT ANYMORE.
End Chapter Six.

Spring, 1962...
...the French Quarter...
...New Orleans, Louisiana.
IT MAY BE TRUE THAT, AS JFK SAID, "THE TORCH HAS BEEN PASSED TO A NEW GENERATION..."
...BUT WHEN IT COMES TO MARDI GRAS, IT'S BASICALLY THE SAME SHIT THIS YEAR AND EVERY YEAR...
...PERFECTLY RESPECTABLE ASSHOLES FROM ALL OVER AMERICA AND THE WORLD...
...BEHAVING LIKE DRUNKEN HOOLIGANS AND OUT-OF-CONTROL SLUTS...
...AS LONG AS THEY THINK NOBODY WHO GIVES A DAMN IS LOOKING.
BEVERLY AND DAGMAR MAY APPEAR TO BE OUT-OF-CONTROL SLUTS...
BUT IN THIS CASE, THEY'RE ONLY DOING IT FOR THE MOVIES.
OKAY, NOW KISS-- LOTSA TONGUE THERE...
EUNICE MacAVOY FIRST APPEARED ON SCREEN IN 1919...
...Y'KNOW, LIKE YER MORE THAN FRIENDS, RIGHT...

...FOR A BRIEF AND VERY MINOR CAREER IN MOTION PICTURES, MOSTLY PORTRAYING FALLEN WOMEN IN MOVIES LONG LOST TO DETERIORATION.
...THAT'S RIGHT--
--NOW GIVE ME A LITTLE CUNT BUMP AND HUMP--
--AND CUT!
62

YOU WANT TO TIGHTEN YOUR GAFF A BIT, HONEY...
...I COULD FEEL YOU SQUIRMING AROUND IN THERE.
I KNOW, I KNOW--
...WHICH IS NOT TO SAY, OF COURSE, THAT I'M NOT INCREDIBLY FLATTERED...
...KNOWING I STILL GET YOU HARD AS A ROCK.
YOU'RE MAKING ME BLUSH, LIKE ALWAYS.
AND THAT'S ONLY ONE OF THE REASONS I LOVE YOU...
...AFTER ALL THESE YEARS, YOU'RE STILL THE PERFECT BLEND OF VIRGIN AND WHORE.
WHEN SOUND CAME IN, EUNICE CHANGED EVERYTHING ABOUT HER LOOK AND BECAME ILONA FONTAINE, A '30S GLAMORPUSS WITH NO TALENT...

...ONLY TO HAVE ILONA DISAPPEAR SOMEWHERE IN THE MID-ATLANTIC IN LATE 1939...
THAT'S RIGHT, BEV...
...TO BE REPLACED BY BLANCHE DeWOLFE, CABARET STAR AND THE RISQUE TOAST OF PARIS.
...THEY'RE ALL GONNA WANT A PIECE O' THAT SWEET ASS...
BLANCHE DIED TRAGICALLY DURING THE LIBERATION OF PARIS...
...SO LET'S SHAKE THOSE TITS AND GIVE EVERYBODY OUT THERE IN THE DARK THEIR MONEY'S WORTH.
FOR YOU, MOE, ANYTHING...
HELL WITH THAT LITTLE JEW, HONEY...
...HOW 'BOUT SOME O' THAT 'ANYTHING FOR YOU' WITH A REAL MAN?
IF THAT MEANS YOU, HAP...
...I'LL STICK WITH FUCKING THE LITTLE JEW.

...AND BEVERLY GROVE SHOWED UP ON THE SAG MEMBERSHIP ROLL SOMETIME IN LATE 1955...
...WITH NO MORE TALENT THAN SHE'D SHOWN IN ANY OF HER PREVIOUS INCARNATIONS.
FUCKING CUNT.
NO SHIT.
IF IT AIN'T KIKES...
...IT'S NIGGERS.
NO SHIT.
GETTIN' T'BE SO A WHITE MAN CAN'T WET HIS DICK IN A WHITE PUSSY 'THOUT GETTIN' IN LINE.
AND DON'T FORGET THE SPICS AND THE WOPS.
FUCK THOSE WHITE TRASH ASSHOLES.
REALLY?
WHAT ABOUT THAT LITTLE SURPRISE OF YOURS?
I DID.
UH HUH--
I WAS ON THE RAG.
LONGEST PERIOD IN HISTORY.
YEP--
--AND TO TELL YOU THE GOD'S HONEST TRUTH...
...I GOT THE FEELING I WAS JUST AN EXCUSE FOR HAP AND AL THERE TO GET, Y'KNOW, INTIMATE WITH EACH OTHER.

TWO GOOD OL' BOYS JUST WANT TO FUCK AND BE FUCKED, AND TOO SCARED TO COME CLEAN ABOUT IT.
SOUNDS LIKE MY KIND OF PARTY, LADIES.
CLAY, DARLIN'--
--YOU REMEMBER MY BEST GIRLFRIEND, BEVERLY...?
I DO INDEED. I'M A BIG FAN OF ALL YOUR PICTURES, MISS GROVE...
...YOU SURE YOU WON'T JOIN US?
YOU'RE VERY KIND, BUT I THINK DAGMAR DESERVES A BIT OF UNDIVIDED ATTENTION, DON'T YOU?
SEE YOU LATER, BEV...
...AND DON'T WAIT UP.
HEY, DOLLFACE--
TAKE A HIKE, FAGGOT...
...CAN'T YOU SEE I'M BUSY WITH SOME REAL MEN?
QUESTION FOR THEM IS...
...WHERE'S THIS PARTY GOING, TIGER?

CLAY SHAW IS A NOTORIOUS MOVER AND SHAKER IN NEW ORLEANS...
...WITH ENOUGH DIRT ON THOSE THAT CARE ABOUT SUCH THINGS TO GET AWAY WITH ANYTHING SHORT OF MURDER.
THAT'S RIGHT, CLAY, HONEY...
...THAT MAY NOT BE THE FIRST DICK YOU'VE SUCKED...
...BUT I'M BETTIN' IT'S THE FIRST ONE ON A BLONDE WITH TITS OUT TO THERE, HUH?
I CAN TELL HOW MUCH YOU'RE LOVIN' THIS, LEE...
...SO QUIT YER SQUIRMIN'...
OH GODOHGOD OHGOD--
...OR ELSE I'M LIABLE TO ACCIDENTALLY TURN YOU INSIDE OUT.
Mmmm ...ahh FUCK--
--I JUST CAME...
THEN YOU BETTER CLEAN IT UP AND EAT IT...

"...CAUSE I SURE AIN'T GONNA DO IT."
OKAY, BOYS...
SAME WOMAN. SAME FACE. SAME BODY.
DIFFERENT NAME. DIFFERENT HAIR. DIFFERENT MAKEUP.
IT MAY HAVE BEEN THE INSIGNIFICANCE OF THE VARIOUS CAREERS...
...OR SIMPLY CULTURAL AMNESIA...
...YOU WANT THIS TIGHT WHITE PUSSY...
...THAT ALLOWED HER TO SLIP THROUGH THE CRACKS...
...I'VE GOT TO SEE SOME SERIOUS BLACK DICK.
THIS WORTH GETTIN' KILLED FOR?
YOU STUCK AROUND WHEN THAT CRACKER ASSHOLE CAME BY...
YEAH, BUT I NEVER EXPECTED IT TO GO THIS FAR.
YOU WANNA TALK OR FUCK?
NOW THAT'S WHAT I LIKE TO SEE--
--WHITE GIRL KNOWS WHAT'S GOOD FOR HER.

...BUT WHATEVER THE REASON, BEVERLY, a.k.a. BLANCHE a.k.a. ILONA, nee EUNICE...
I WANT EVERY HOLE PACKED WITH BLACK COCK--
--AND I WANT IT NOW, YOU MOTHERFUCKERS!
...HAS MANAGED TO MAINTAIN FOUR DIFFERENT CAREERS...
...IN THE PUBLIC'S EYE...
...WITH REMARKABLY FEW NOTICING THEY WERE LOOKING AT THE SAME WOMAN FOR OVER FOUR DECADES.
AND, OF COURSE, WITH VERY FEW EXCEPTIONS...
...THOSE WHO DID NOTICE ENDED UP SERIOUSLY FUCKED...
...AND BRUTALLY, BLOODILY DEAD.
I COULDN'T'VE BEEN HAPPIER THAT YOU BOYS STOOD UP TO THOSE REDNECK PECKERWOODS TONIGHT...

...BECAUSE THIS GIRL NEEDED SOME SERIOUS FUCKING...
...FROM SOME SERIOUS DICK...
...AND THOSE TWO'D RATHER FUCK EACH OTHER THAN ME.
THEY JUST DON'T KNOW HOW TO OWN UP TO IT YET.
AND FROM THE MOMENT THAT THIS INSATIABLE SUCCUBUS FOUND HER FIRST THRALL...
AND SINCE WE'VE GOT TWO MORE DAYS OF PICKUP SHOTS WITH THEM...
WHAT THE FUCK!!?
...HER LIFE BECAME QUANTITATIVELY EASIER AND MORE SATISFYING.
...HAP AND AL'D BE MISSED A LOT MORE THAN YOU THREE WILL...
WITH A TWIN FOR COMPANY...
...IF YOU GET MY GIST.

I JUST CAN'T *IMAGINE* WHAT KIND OF *GIRL* YOU THINK I AM...
...*TRULY*, I CAN'T.
...AND FOR PLAYFUL, GIRLISH CONFUSION, TOO.
NOW WHY DON'T YOU JUST SIT *DOWN*, DADDY...
...WHILE I SLIP INTO SOMETHING MORE *COMFORTABLE?*
YOU WANNA GIVE IT A *MINUTE*, SWEETIE...
...THEY'RE *MORONS*, BUT EVEN *MOE* WON'T EXPECT *THAT* QUICK A COSTUME CHANGE.
METAIRIE RENTALS, IN
I'VE BEEN THROUGH THIS *BEFORE*, DAG--
--I KNOW MY WAY *AROUND*--
--AND *THANKS* FOR COVERING MY *ASS*...
...*THIS'LL* KEEP ANY OVEREAGER *HOMICIDE* DICK CONFUSED LONG ENOUGH TO STOP *BOTHERING*.
'S'WHY I'M *HERE*, DOLL.
WELL, *WELL...*
...DON'T *YOU* LOOK GOOD ENOUGH TO *EAT*...
End Chapter Seven.

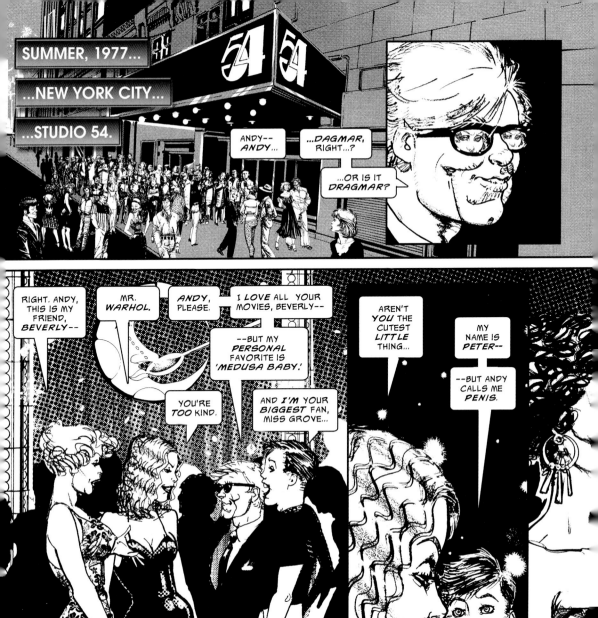

SUMMER, 1977...

...NEW YORK CITY...

...STUDIO 54.

ANDY-- ANDY...

...DAGMAR, RIGHT...?

...OR IS IT DRAGMAR?

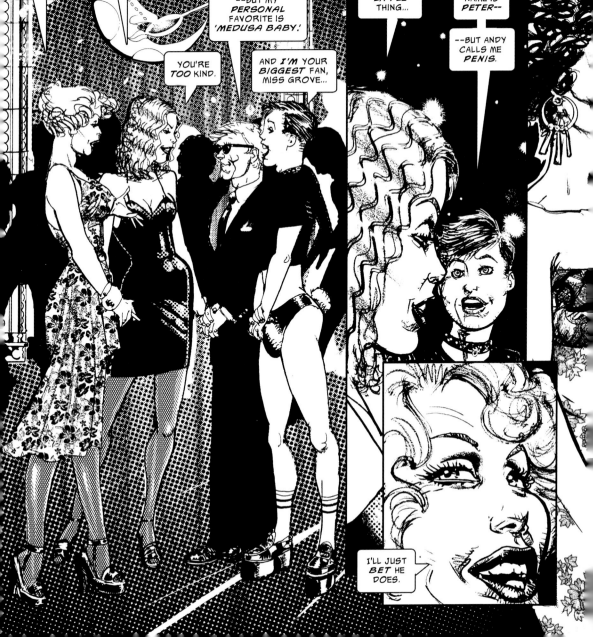

RIGHT. ANDY, THIS IS MY FRIEND, BEVERLY--

MR. WARHOL.

ANDY, PLEASE.

I LOVE ALL YOUR MOVIES, BEVERLY--

--BUT MY PERSONAL FAVORITE IS 'MEDUSA BABY.'

YOU'RE TOO KIND.

AND I'M YOUR BIGGEST FAN, MISS GROVE...

AREN'T YOU THE CUTEST LITTLE THING...

MY NAME IS PETER--

--BUT ANDY CALLS ME PENIS.

I'LL JUST BET HE DOES.

IS ANDY ALWAYS LIKE THAT?
LIKE WHAT?
LIKE THAT.
OH, YES-- THAT'S THE REAL THING.
ANDY SAYS HE'D KILL TO HAVE YOU DO HIS NEXT MOVIE, BEV.
THAT WOULD BE FABULOUS...
ANDY'S A GENIUS, AND SO ARE YOU.
OH, PLEASE.
I MADE A STRING OF SHITTY LITTLE MOVIES FOR NO MONEY...
...AIMED AT MASTURBATING RETARDS.
HEY--
--GENIUS COMES IN ALL SHAPES AND SIZES, RIGHT, DAGMAR?
YOU SAID IT, PENIS.
THAT'S PETER, TO YOU...

IT'S BEEN A GOOD RUN FOR BEVERLY AND DAGMAR...
...ONLY ANDY GETS TO CALL ME PENIS.
...DAGMAR II, TO BE EXACT.
TWENTY YEARS, ALMOST TO THE DAY.
THEY'VE BEEN ALL OVER THE WORLD...
...FUCKING, SUCKING AND INCIDENTALLY MURDERING THEIR WAY THROUGH LIFE.
YOU'RE MUCH MORE BEAUTIFUL THAN I COULD EVER HAVE IMAGINED.
OH, COME ON...
...THAT'S EASY TO SAY WHEN THE LIGHTS ARE OUT.

NO, REALLY, I MEAN IT-- TRULY I DO.
YOU'VE BEEN MY IDOL FOR SO LONG--
NOTHING A GIRL LIKES MORE THAN BEING REMINDED SHE'S OLDER THAN DIRT.
THAT'S NOT WHAT I MEAN, AND YOU KNOW IT.
YOU'RE FUCKING GORGEOUS.
THAT'S VERY KIND OF YOU, BUT REALLY NOW, AND NO OFFENSE...
...BUT IN THAT OUTFIT, I'D HARDLY CALL YOU THE BEST JUDGE OF FEMALE BEAUTY, IF YOU KNOW WHAT I MEAN.
DON'T LET MY LOOKS FOOL YOU...
...I'LL FUCK AND BE FUCKED BY ANYTHING OR ANYONE WITH HAIR WHO'S NOT DEAD--
SPREADING YOURSELF A LITTLE THIN THERE, AREN'T YOU?
GOT THAT RIGHT.
THAT'S PETER-- AS IN PETER PAN-SEXUAL.
SO MAYBE THERE IS MORE TO YOU THAN JUST A NELLY IN GLITTER AND HEELS.

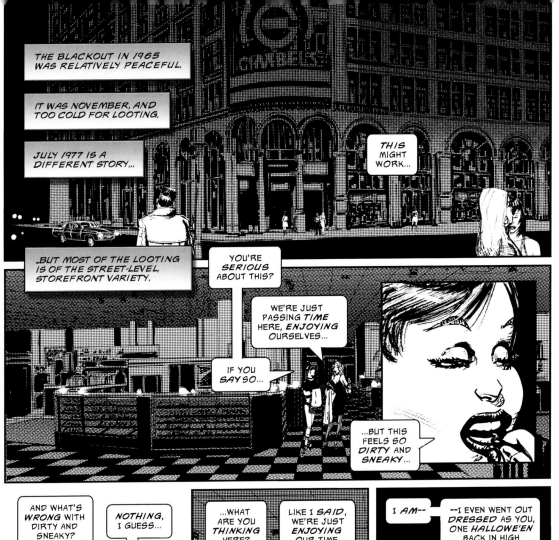

THE BLACKOUT IN 1965 WAS RELATIVELY PEACEFUL.

IT WAS NOVEMBER, AND TOO COLD FOR LOOTING.

JULY 1977 IS A DIFFERENT STORY...

THIS MIGHT WORK...

...BUT MOST OF THE LOOTING IS OF THE STREET-LEVEL, STOREFRONT VARIETY.

YOU'RE SERIOUS ABOUT THIS?

WE'RE JUST PASSING TIME HERE, ENJOYING OURSELVES...

IF YOU SAY SO...

...BUT THIS FEELS SO DIRTY AND SNEAKY...

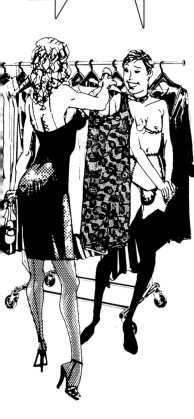

AND WHAT'S WRONG WITH DIRTY AND SNEAKY?

NOTHING, I GUESS...

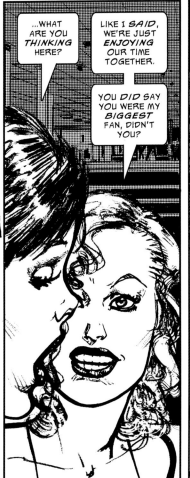

...WHAT ARE YOU THINKING HERE?

LIKE I SAID, WE'RE JUST ENJOYING OUR TIME TOGETHER.

YOU DID SAY YOU WERE MY BIGGEST FAN, DIDN'T YOU?

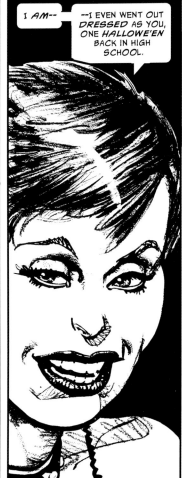

I AM--

--I EVEN WENT OUT DRESSED AS YOU, ONE HALLOWE'EN BACK IN HIGH SCHOOL.

"THEN WHAT COULD BE MORE PERFECT?"
WHERE THE FUCK'VE YOU BEEN?
I'VE BEEN WORRIED SICK
SPARE ME, DAGMAR...
...THE ONLY THING YOU EVER WORRY ABOUT IS HOW YOUR FAT ASS LOOKS IN TIGHT JEANS.
I DO EVERYTHING I CAN TO MAKE YOU HAPPY...
AND THAT'S WHY YOU'RE STILL BREATHING...
...INSTEAD OF BEING ON THE BOOKS AS ONE MORE UNSOLVED FAG MURDER IN VANAHEIM.
YOU SAYING I'M NOT GRATEFUL FOR EVERYTHING?
NO--
--I'M SAYING YOUR WHINING IS GETTING ON MY NERVES.

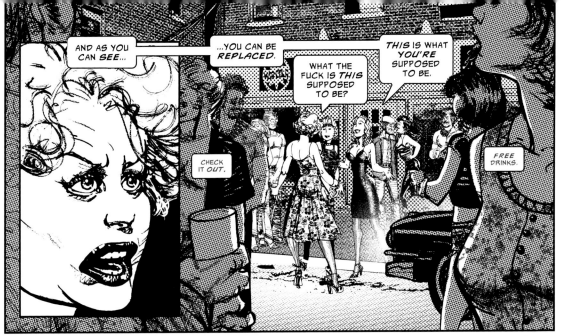

AND AS YOU CAN SEE...

...YOU CAN BE REPLACED.

WHAT THE FUCK IS THIS SUPPOSED TO BE?

THIS IS WHAT YOU'RE SUPPOSED TO BE.

CHECK IT OUT.

FREE DRINKS.

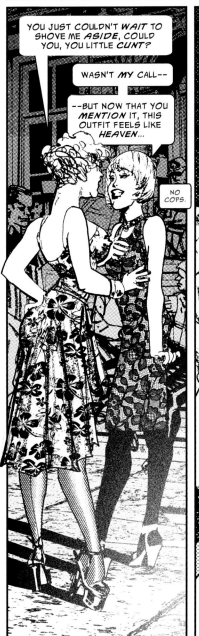

YOU JUST COULDN'T WAIT TO SHOVE ME ASIDE, COULD YOU, YOU LITTLE CUNT?

WASN'T MY CALL--

--BUT NOW THAT YOU MENTION IT, THIS OUTFIT FEELS LIKE HEAVEN...

NO COPS.

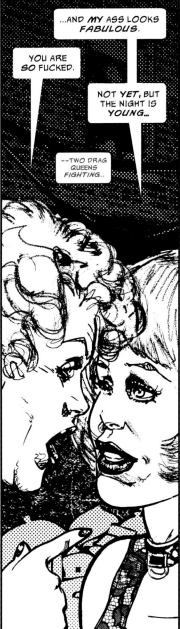

...AND MY ASS LOOKS FABULOUS.

YOU ARE SO FUCKED.

NOT YET, BUT THE NIGHT IS YOUNG...

--TWO DRAG QUEENS FIGHTING...

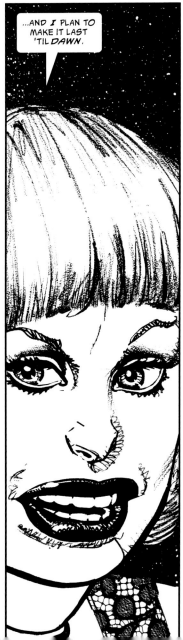

...AND I PLAN TO MAKE IT LAST 'TIL DAWN.

FUCKING BITCH--!
THIS SHIT IS PRICELESS!
YOU SAY THAT LIKE IT'S A BAD THING.
IT DOESN'T HAVE TO BE LIKE THIS, DAGMAR.
LIKE SHIT IT DOESN'T.
YOU MOVED IN ON US LIKE THE SEVEN SANTINI BROTHERS...
FUCK YOU BACK, YOU SKANKY BITCH--
COME ON, FAGGOT, KICK HER ASS.
RANK, OUT!!
--I WAS INVITED.
FUCK YOU, INVITED--
--WHO ASKED YOU TO FUCK UP MY LIFE?

THAT WOULD BE ME.
PSYCH!!
OH,
SNAP!
OH, SHIT.
EXACTLY.
THUNDT!
BUT--
LATER.

LATER...
THAT--
--WAS--
--OFF--
--THE CHARTS--
SHUT UP AND FUCK ME.
BUT--
I ASKED YOU TO SHUT UP.
NOW, YOU CAN HAVE AN INCREDIBLE LIFE, HANGING OUT WITH YOUR FUCKING IDOL DAY AND NIGHT...
...OR I CAN PICK YOU UP AND THROW YOU OFF THIS ROOF...
...AND JUST KEEP LOOKING FOR SOMEONE WHO REALLY WANTS THE JOB.
I'M IN.
FINE. NOW WHAT'S YOUR NAME?
DAGMAR.
END CHAPTER EIGHT.

WINTER, 1984...
...SOUTHERN CALIFORNIA...
...LOS ANGELES.
AHH...
LIKE THA--
--MRPHH...!?
SHUT UP AND KEEP SUCKING, ELLEN...
ELLEN POLLACK'S BEEN MARRIED FOR A YEAR.
RICKY FABRIKANT MARRIED LORETTA SIX YEARS AGO.
Musso & Fran
...I KNEW THAT MOUTH OF YOURS WAS WASTED ON YOUR FUCKING LOWLIFE HUSBAND.
MRPHH...
I DON'T NEED YOU TO BRING CASS UP--
I SAID SHUT UP AND SUCK, YOU LITTLE WHORE...
MRRPPHHH...
YOU WANNA MAKE NOISE, JUST HUM.

BARELY TEN MILES AWAY, BUT LIGHT YEARS DISTANT IN SO MANY WAYS...
...THE SAN FERNANDO VALLEY...
...STUDIO CITY...
GO AHEAD—
...VENTURA BOULEVARD.
CASS AND ELLEN POLLACK HAVE THEIR ISSUES...
—SAY IT.
OH, COME ON--
CHEZ BOP
...NOT THE LEAST OF WHICH IS LORETTA FABRIKANT...
SAY IT, OR I'LL FUCK YOU UP.
OOOH-- SCARY, KIDS...
OH, COME ON LORETTA.
FINE.
DESPITE THE FACT HE'S GOT A DICK AS BIG AS MY FOREARM, I'D STILL RATHER HAVE YOUR COCK INSIDE ME.
HAPPY NOW?
HAPPIER.
12.13 AVR
PORTE
PANTIN
21H
Busch
avec la participation de JAZZ HOT

PICO BOULEVARD IS A NICE JEWISH NEIGHBORHOOD ON THE WEST SIDE OF LOS ANGELES...
LARRY--!
OH, FUCK, MAN--
--WHY?
YOU GOTTA ASK...
PAWN
ON RE
....THEN IT'S CLEAR SOMEBODY ISN'T PAYING ATTENTION, 'M I RIGHT, MR. FISH?
TOO TRUE, NUNZ, TOO TRUE.
I SAID I'D COVER IT, MR. FISH--
TOO LITTLE, TOO LATE, VARADI...
--IT HURTS SO MUCH!
...AND LIKE THEY SAY IN THE CARTOONS, 'YOU KNEW THE JOB WAS DANGEROUS WHEN YOU TOOK IT.'
PLEASE...
EASY NOW, BITCH, AND SHUT THE FUCK UP...
...YOU KNOW YOU LOVED THAT BIG BLACK DICK UP YOUR SWEET WHITE ASS.
NOW GET THAT DICK GOOD AND CLEAN--
--LAST THING I WANT IS JIZ ON MY NEW SUIT, RIGHT?
SEE THAT, VARADI?
JUST BE GRATEFUL CLADYS THERE DIDN'T MAKE YOU AND THAT LITTLE WIFE OF YOURS CLEAN IT OFF TOGETHER.

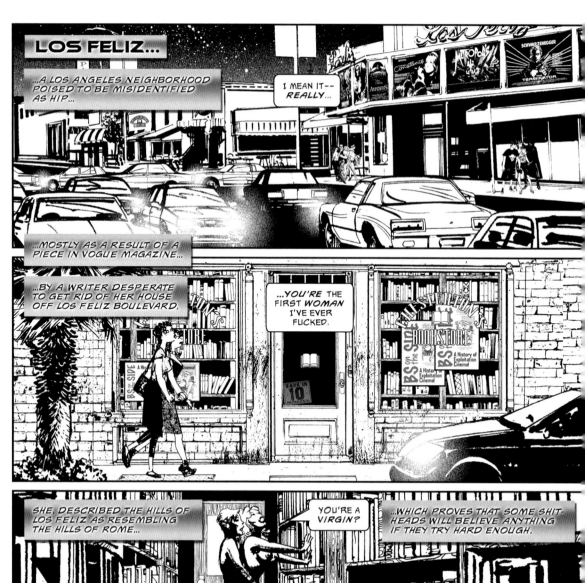

LOS FELIZ...

...A LOS ANGELES NEIGHBORHOOD POISED TO BE MISIDENTIFIED AS HIP...

I MEAN IT-- REALLY...

...MOSTLY AS A RESULT OF A PIECE IN VOGUE MAGAZINE...

...BY A WRITER DESPERATE TO GET RID OF HER HOUSE OFF LOS FELIZ BOULEVARD.

...YOU'RE THE FIRST WOMAN I'VE EVER FUCKED.

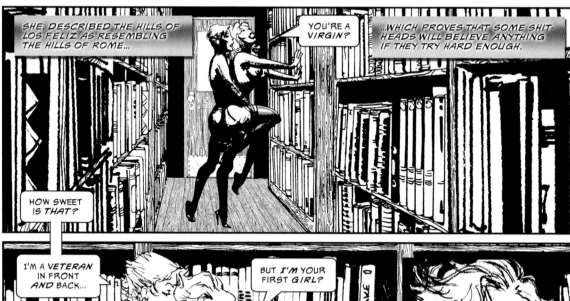

SHE, DESCRIBED THE HILLS OF LOS FELIZ AS RESEMBLING THE HILLS OF ROME...

YOU'RE A VIRGIN?

...WHICH PROVES THAT SOME SHIT-HEADS WILL BELIEVE ANYTHING IF THEY TRY HARD ENOUGH.

HOW SWEET IS THAT?

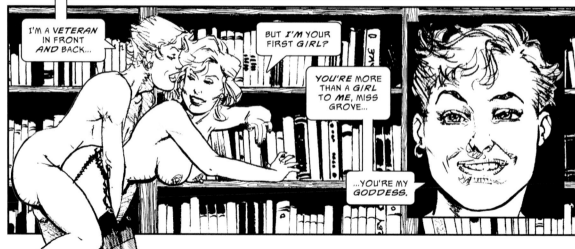

I'M A VETERAN IN FRONT AND BACK...

BUT I'M YOUR FIRST GIRL?

YOU'RE MORE THAN A GIRL TO ME, MISS GROVE...

...YOU'RE MY GODDESS.

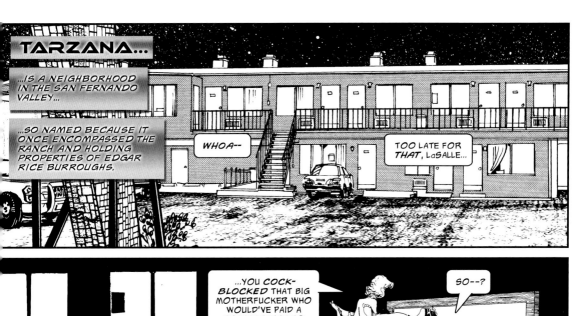

TARZANA...

...IS A NEIGHBORHOOD IN THE SAN FERNANDO VALLEY...

...SO NAMED BECAUSE IT ONCE ENCOMPASSED THE RANCH AND HOLDING PROPERTIES OF EDGAR RICE BURROUGHS.

WHOA--

TOO LATE FOR *THAT*, LaSALLE...

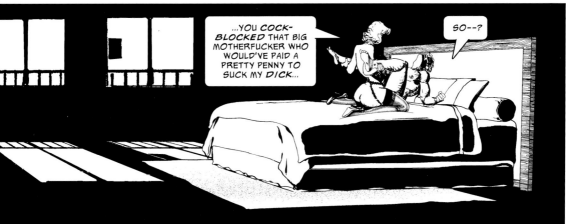

...YOU *COCK-BLOCKED* THAT BIG MOTHERFUCKER WHO WOULD'VE PAID A PRETTY PENNY TO SUCK MY *DICK*...

SO--?

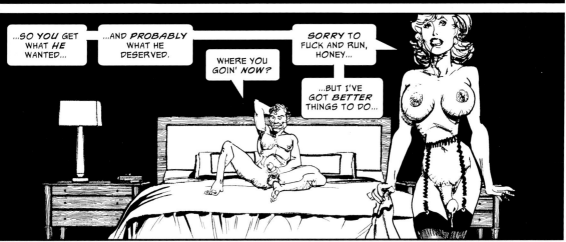

...SO *YOU* GET WHAT *HE* WANTED...

...AND *PROBABLY* WHAT HE DESERVED.

WHERE YOU GOIN' *NOW*?

SORRY TO FUCK AND RUN, HONEY...

...BUT I'VE GOT *BETTER* THINGS TO DO...

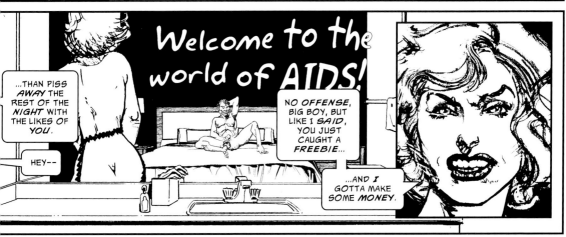

Welcome to the world of AIDS!

...THAN PISS *AWAY* THE REST OF THE *NIGHT* WITH THE LIKES OF *YOU*.

HEY--

NO OFFENSE, BIG BOY, BUT LIKE I *SAID*, YOU JUST CAUGHT A *FREEBIE*...

...AND *I* GOTTA MAKE SOME *MONEY*.

SOUTHERN CALIFORNIA, AND LOS ANGELES IN PARTICULAR, HAS LONG BEEN REGARDED AS A CULTURAL WASTELAND...
...BY THE HALF-BLIND THINKERS...
NOT HERE, CASS, FOR CHRIST'S SAKE--
...WHO CAN ONLY DEFINE CULTURE THROUGH AN ANGLO-EUROCENTRIC SCRIM.
PASTRY CAKES
CONTINENTI'S
SPUMONI
--ELLEN'LL BE OUT OF THE BATHROOM ANY SECOND.
AND THAT'S WHAT TABLE TOPS ARE FOR...
...KEEPING YOUR HANDS INVISIBLE FROM EVERYBODY ELSE.
TO THIS WAY OF THINKING, PEOPLE LIKE JOHN LAUTNER AND THE EAMESES WERE ANOMALIES...
COUNT TO THIRTY, THEN MAKE LIKE YOU JUST GOT HERE.
FUCK THAT.
...AS OPPOSED TO THE VANGUARD OF THE SECOND HALF OF THE AMERICAN CENTURY'S CULTURAL SENSIBILITY.
LOOK WHO I RAN INTO.
CLADYS--ALWAYS A TREAT, NEVER A TREATMENT.
THAT SUPPOSED TO BE FUNNY, FAGGOT?

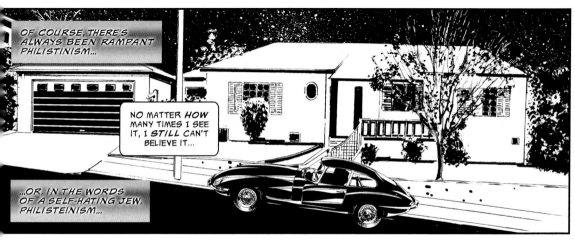

OF COURSE, THERE'S ALWAYS BEEN RAMPANT PHILISTINISM...

NO MATTER *HOW* MANY TIMES I SEE IT, I *STILL* CAN'T BELIEVE IT...

...OR, IN THE WORDS OF A SELF-HATING JEW, PHILISTEINISM...

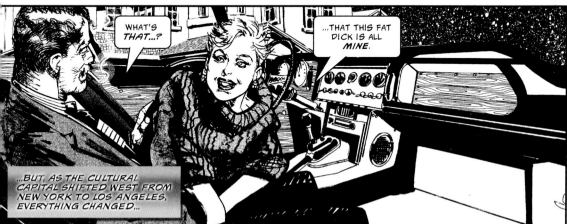

WHAT'S *THAT*...?

...THAT THIS FAT DICK IS ALL *MINE.*

...BUT, AS THE CULTURAL CAPITAL SHIFTED WEST FROM NEW YORK TO LOS ANGELES, EVERYTHING CHANGED...

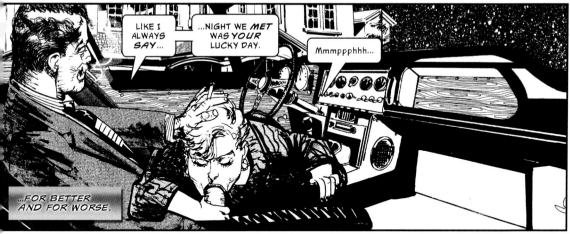

LIKE I ALWAYS *SAY*...

...NIGHT WE *MET* WAS *YOUR* LUCKY DAY.

Mmmppphhh...

...FOR BETTER AND FOR WORSE.

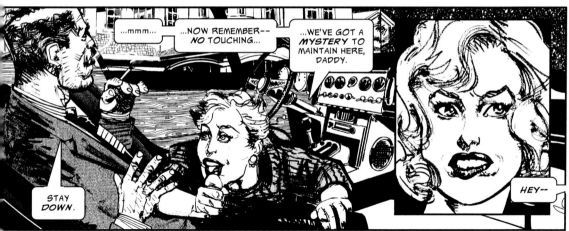

...mmm...

...NOW REMEMBER-- NO TOUCHING...

...WE'VE GOT A *MYSTERY* TO MAINTAIN HERE, DADDY.

STAY *DOWN.*

HEY--

DAGMAR, RIGHT?
WHO'S ASKING?
DETECTIVE FABRIKANT, LAPD...
...AND IF YOU ARE DAGMAR PETERS, I HAVE A FEW QUESTIONS.
ME TOO, OFFICER--
--IS THAT A PISTOL IN YOUR POCKET, OR ARE YOU JUST GLAD TO SEE ME?
BLAM!
IT'S A PISTOL.
BLAM!
THANK YOU, DADDY...
...THAT'S THE BEST BIRTHDAY PRESENT A GIRL COULD EVER ASK FOR.

SANTA VARDA...

...IS A LITTLE COASTAL TOWN JUST AN HOUR NORTH OF LOS ANGELES...

...AN HOUR NORTH, BUT A DIFFERENT WORLD OF HAVES AND HAVE-NOTS.

...THE *VICTIM* IS DESCRIBED AS A *TRANSVESTITE,* BORN PETER LANGAN, 28 YEARS OF AGE...

...NEIGHBORS, WHO REFUSED TO BE *IDENTIFIED*...

IT'S A TOWN WITH NO MIDDLE CLASS...

...JUST A MINORITY OF WEALTHY CLIFF AND BEACH DWELLERS...

...SAY MR. LANGAN ENTERTAINED *VISITORS* AT ALL HOURS...

...SERVED BY A MAJORITY OF MEXICANS, GUATEMALANS AND COLOMBIANS...

...CHARGED WITH RAISING THE GRANDEES' CHILDREN, MAINTAINING THEIR LAWNS, AND CLEANING THEIR HOMES.

nok nok

I CAME AS SOON AS I HEARD.

I NEVER *KNEW* HER, OF *COURSE*....

...BUT FROM *EVERYTHING* YOU'VE TOLD ME, I KNOW JUST HOW *MUCH* DAGMAR *MEANT* TO YOU.

THAT'S VERY *SWEET*...

...BUT WHEN YOU'VE BEEN *AROUND* AS LONG AS *I* HAVE...

...SUDDEN LOSS IS JUST PART OF LIFE.
I THOUGHT YOU MIGHT NOT WANT TO BE ALONE TONIGHT.
HOW THOUGHTFUL OF YOU, DANNY...
...HOW INCREDIBLY THOUGHTFUL.
DON'T MENTION IT.
I WON'T MENTION IT AGAIN...
SANTA VARDA...
...IT'S ALL ABOUT SERVICE.
...AND I WON'T MENTION THE LATENT SMELL OF CORDITE RESIDUE STILL ON YOUR CLOTHES.
CALL ME BEVERLY.
I JUST CAN'T IMAGINE WHAT YOU MEAN, MISS GROVE...
PERFECT...
...AND YOU CAN CALL ME DAGMAR.
END CHAPTER NINE.

WINTER, 1991...
...THE STRIP...
...LAS VEGAS, NEVADA.
IT WAS THE EARLY '80S WHEN THE MORMON HYPOCRITES WHO RUN LAS VEGAS FOR THE SYNDICATE MADE THE DECISION...
...TO TRANSFORM THEIR DESERT TOWN FROM AN OASIS OF SLEAZE...
...TO A FAMILY-FRIENDLY ENTERTAINMENT DESTINATION.
WELCOME EXPOROTICA '91
SHOW US YOUR TITS!
ASSHOLE'S IN THE WRONG ROOM.
I DON'T KNOW—
--I WOULDN'T MIND SEEING HER TITS.
I HAVE...
...AND THEY'RE NOTHING TO WRITE HOME ABOUT.
THE MORMONS' OUTFIT PARTNERS WENT FOR THE CLEAN UP, TOO...
DEPENDS ON WHERE YOU CALL HOME.
I HAD HER, TOO, AND CASS IS RIGHT ON.
SHE'S ONE OF THOSE CHICKS...
...FOR HER, GREAT SEX IS JUST SHOWING UP.
WORD ON THAT—
FUCK YOU GOING?

...I'LL BE BACK FOR THE THIRD SET.
...BUT THERE'S SOME SLEAZE THAT JUST WILL NOT GO AWAY.
MAN--WAS SHE HOT, OR WHAT?
KEEP WALKING.
YOU A FAN?
WHAT'D I SAY, RIGHT? FUCK OFF.
THAT ANY WAY TO TALK TO YOUR PUBLIC?
AREN'T WE FEELING PHILOSOPHICAL TODAY?
THAT WHY YOU SNEAKED OFF THE BANDSTAND BEFORE THE SET WAS OVER?
FUCKING SUE RATTED ME OUT?
ACTUALLY, SHE TRIED TO COVER FOR YOU...
I DON'T HAVE A PUBLIC, ROSEMARY.
THAT WAS JUST ONE MORE MOUTH-BREATHER WHO'D RATHER SPEND TIME ALONE WITH HIS FIST AND A DREAM...
...RATHER THAN TAKE A CHANCE ON BEING DISAPPOINTED BY SWEATY, SMELLY REALITY.

AND ANYWAY, THE SYNDICATE HAD SO MUCH DRUG MONEY FLOATING AROUND...
...I JUST HAPPENED TO STICK MY NOSE IN AND CAUGHT YOU TIPPING OUT.
TALENT BOOKER KEEPING AN EYE ON TALENT...
YEAH--ALMOST SOUNDS LIKE CHEATING, HUH?
...THERE WAS NO WAY THE FAMILIES WERE GOING TO GIVE UP THE BEST MONEY-LAUNDERING SCHEME THEY EVER HAD...
SO--
--FREAKED OUT AT ALL THE BEVERLY SHIT, HUH?
AND YOU'RE NOT?
...BURYING HEROIN, MARIJUANA AND CRACK PROFITS...
I'M NOT THRILLED, BUT THREE YEARS OF THERAPY HAVE HELPED A LOT.
...IN THE ADULT FILM INDUSTRY.
WISH I COULD SAY THE SAME...

...BUT THEN AGAIN, DOUBLING DOWN ON MY DRINKING PROBABLY DOESN'T REALLY COUNT AS THERAPY.
YOU SAY SOMETHING?
NO-- SORRY.
HEY--I CAUGHT YOUR ACT...
...AND YOU'RE NOT BAD ON THE TENOR.
THANKS--
NO, REALLY, I MEAN IT...
...I HEARD A LITTLE HAWK AND A TOUCH OF PRES BACK THERE.
MAN--
--YOU ACTUALLY KNOW WHAT YOU'RE TALKING ABOUT.
NO NEED TO SOUND SO SURPRISED, HONEY.
NOT SURPRISED AT ALL...
...TRUTH IS, I'VE ALWAYS KNOWN...
...SHOW ME AN ATTRACTIVE WOMAN WHO DIGS JAZZ...
...AND I'LL SHOW YOU A TRANSVESTITE.

THANKS FOR NOTHING, ASSHOLE.
THE MORMONS...
...AND THE REST OF THE WORLD THAT SEES PORN AS A SIN...
...OPERATE UNDER THE IMPRESSION THAT IT SHOWS A BIG PROFIT.
EXPOROTICA '91
IT CAN HAPPEN...
THE TRUTH IS THAT PORN TURNS NO PROFIT WHATSOEVER.
THE MONEY IS IN DRUGS AND PROSTITUTION...
...AND PORN IS THE PERFECT PLACE TO HIDE THE WINDFALL PROFITS OF THOSE ILLICIT ENTERPRISES...
WE CAN DO IT.
THE DREAM STILL LIVES...
...IN THE ZERO-SUM GAME OF DIRECT-TO-VIDEO SLEAZE.
NONE OF THIS MEANS SHIT TO A TREE TO CASS POLLACK...
...A GUY WHO'S BEEN THROUGH THE MILL CALLED BEVERLY GROVE...
...AND SHOULD KNOW WELL ENOUGH TO STAY THE FUCK AWAY.

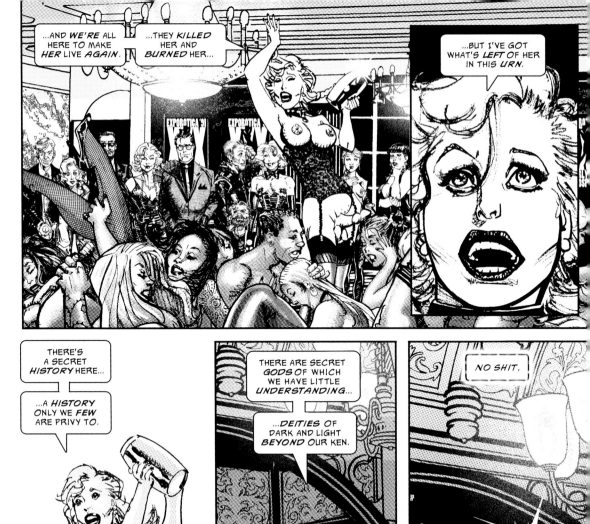

...AND *WE'RE* ALL HERE TO MAKE *HER* LIVE *AGAIN*.

...THEY *KILLED* HER AND *BURNED* HER...

...BUT I'VE GOT WHAT'S *LEFT* OF HER IN THIS *URN*.

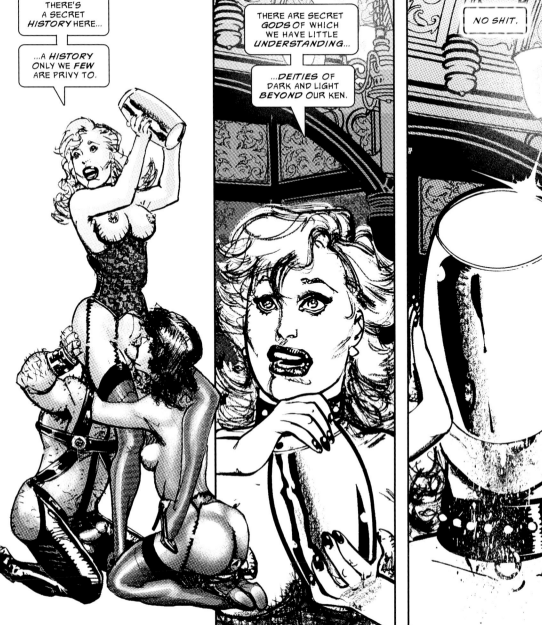

THERE'S A SECRET *HISTORY* HERE...

...A *HISTORY* ONLY WE *FEW* ARE PRIVY TO.

THERE ARE SECRET *GODS* OF WHICH WE HAVE LITTLE *UNDERSTANDING*...

...*DEITIES* OF DARK AND LIGHT *BEYOND* OUR KEN.

NO SHIT.

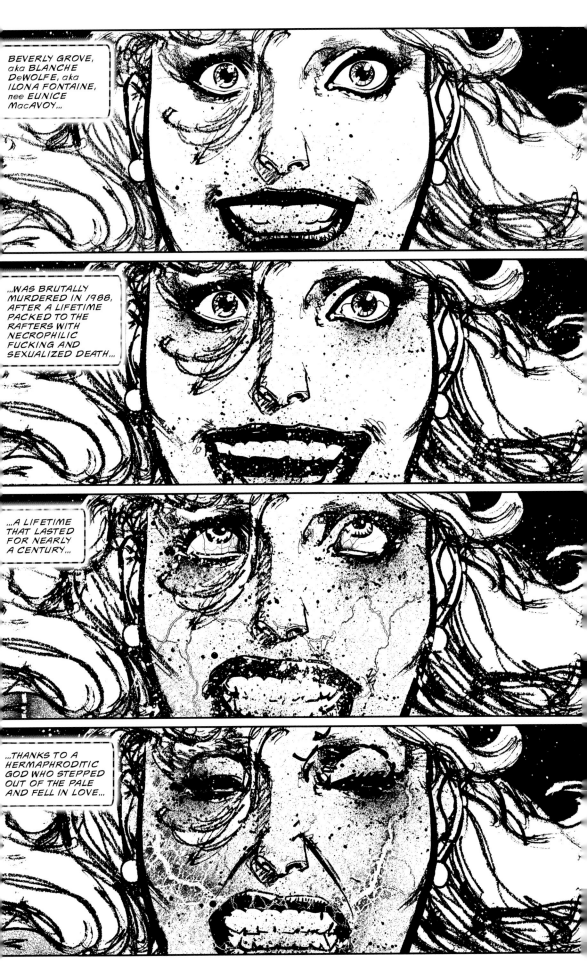

BEVERLY GROVE,
aka BLANCHE
DeWOLFE, aka
ILONA FONTAINE,
nee EUNICE
MacAVOY...

...WAS BRUTALLY
MURDERED IN 1988,
AFTER A LIFETIME
PACKED TO THE
RAFTERS WITH
NECROPHILIC
FUCKING AND
SEXUALIZED DEATH...

...A LIFETIME
THAT LASTED
FOR NEARLY
A CENTURY...

...THANKS TO A
HERMAPHRODITIC
GOD WHO STEPPED
OUT OF THE PALE
AND FELL IN LOVE...

HOLY *FUCK*...

NO *SHIT*, honey...

'S'IS THE *GREATEST*, OR WHAT?

...I GOTTA GET THE *FUCK* OUT OF HERE.

...IN LOVE, NOT WITH MAN, NOR WOMAN, NOR BEAST...

...IN LOVE WITH A DARK PLACE, STROBOSCOPICALLY ILLUMINATED WITH THE FLICKER OF LIGHT AND DARKNESS...

...WITH A SHARED BREATH, A COMMON SHRIEK, A MUTUAL SIGH...

...IN LOVE WITH THE MOVIES.

FUCK ME.
KISS ME ONCE...
...KISS ME TWICE...
...AND KISS ME ONCE AGAIN...
THE BITCH IS BACK.
...IT'S BEEN A LONG, LONG TIME...

WHERE THE FUCK'VE *YOU* BEEN?
WHY *SHOULD—*
SHE'S *BACK.*
FUCK *THAT,* ROSEMARY, AND GET THE *CAR--*
I'LL BE DOWN IN *FIVE* WITH THE *BAGS--*
--AND IF YOU TAKE OFF *WITHOUT* ME, I'LL HUNT YOU DOWN LIKE A *DOG.*
TOOK YOU LONG *ENOUGH.*
YOU *SURE* IT WAS HER?
PLAYERS
WIN BONUSES
WELL, LET'S *SEE*...
...*FIRST* THIS DRAG QUEEN DEAD RINGER FOR *DAGMAR* SWALLOWS AN URN FILLED WITH *SOME-BODY'S* REMAINS...
...AND *THEN,* BEFORE YOU COULD SAY "WE'RE TOTALLY *FUCKED*..."
...*BEVERLY GROVE,* LOOKING *SENSATIONAL* BY THE WAY, *EXPLODES* OUT OF THE TRANNY'S BODY...
...SO *YEAH,* I'D SAY I'M *SURE.*
END CHAPTER TEN.

Late Autumn, 2001...
...San Francisco...
...The Embarcadero.
IN THOSE TERRIBLE, FEAR-FILLED DAYS FOLLOWING THE ATTACKS ON NEW YORK AND WASHINGTON...
...EVERY CITY OF ANY SIZE EXPERIENCED A PAROXYSM OF PARANOIA...
...ALONG WITH A HEALTHY DOLLOP OF WHISTLING-IN-THE-DARK JINGOISM.
CASS POLLACK, NOW CALLING HIMSELF PAUL KASTNER, HAS MORE TO WORRY ABOUT THAN MIDDLE EASTERN TERRORISTS.
THANK YOU, LADIES AND GENTLEMEN...
...I'M VERNA MIRANDE, AND THIS IS MY TRIO...
...AND YOU'VE BEEN A TERRIFIC AUDIENCE.
I'VE HAD BETTER...

...BUT NOT LATELY.
HE'S BEEN ON THE RUN FOR A DECADE...
YOU REALLY ARE A COMPLETE ASSHOLE, YOU KNOW THAT?
I THOUGHT YOU LOVED MY BRUTAL HONESTY.
...CHANGING HIS NAME EVERY FEW MONTHS...
...BUT STUCK MAKING A LIVING THE ONLY WAY HE KNOWS HOW...
YEAH -- BUT NOT WITH YOUR DICK IN ME, FOR CHRIST'S SAKE.
...PLAYING TENOR SAXOPHONE FOR AN AUDIENCE OF SLOWLY DYING JAZZ FANS...
A GIRL LIKES A LITTLE ROMANCE WITH THE FUCKING, IF YOU GET MY MEANING....
YOU WANT ROMANCE, FIND YOURSELF A YOUNGER MAN...
...AND FOR THE DWINDLING CROWD OF RAPIDLY AGING HIPSTERS WHO FIND HIS WORK IRONIC.
JESUS CHRIST, CASS--
--I KNEW YOU WERE FUCKING AROUND--

THE LAST THING CASS POLLACK WANTS OR NEEDS IS ATTENTION...
—BUT WITH THIS SKANKY WHORE?
YOU'VE GOT TO BE SHITTING ME!
YOU NEVER SAID YOU WERE MARRIED--
COME ON, ROSEMARY--
--SHE'S NOT MY WIFE.
NO SHIT--
--BUT YOU'VE BEEN TAKING ADVANTAGE OF MY GOOD NATURE LONG ENOUGH FOR ME TO EXPECT TO BE TREATED LIKE ONE.
WHY DON'T YOU DO US ALL A FAVOR AND FUCK OFF?
...BUT THE SAD SACK ASSHOLE IS STUCK WITH ONLY ONE SALABLE SKILL...
I KEEP RUNNING FOR ONE REASON, AND ONE REASON ONLY--
FOR THE SAME REASON YOU KEEP RUNNING--
--IF THAT BLOOD-SUCKING BITCH CATCHES UP WITH US, WE'RE BOTH FUCKED--
--AND NOT IN A GOOD WAY.

...AND MAKING A LIVING IN PUBLIC...
...EVEN WITH THE CHICKEN-SHIT AUDIENCE HE COMMANDS...
I'M LOOKING FOR SOMEBODY.
...IS HIS ONLY OPTION...
HEY--
...AND BRIMMING WITH RISK.
--EV'BODY'S LOOKIN' FOR SOMEBODY, 'M I RIGHT?
I'M LOOKING FOR A TRANNY WHO WANTS TO BE ME WHEN SHE GROWS UP...
DIVA
THE RISK JUST GOT SERIOUS.
LOOKS LIKE YOURS, THAT COULD BE ANYBODY.
YOU WANT TO CALM DOWN AND STOP WASTING MY TIME, UNLESS YOU PLAN ON GOING BACK TO VAGINATARIANISM...
...THERE'S NO MEAT BETWEEN THESE LEGS.

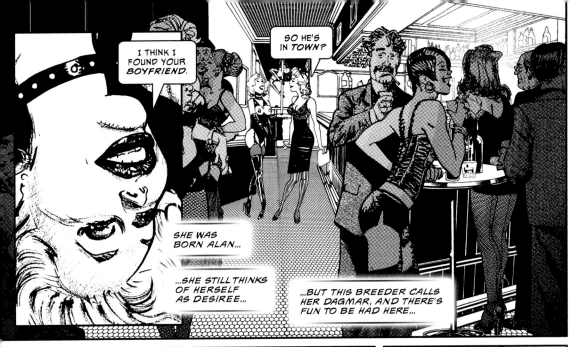

I THINK I FOUND YOUR BOYFRIEND.

SO HE'S IN TOWN?

SHE WAS BORN ALAN...

...SHE STILL THINKS OF HERSELF AS DESIREE...

...BUT THIS BREEDER CALLS HER DAGMAR, AND THERE'S FUN TO BE HAD HERE...

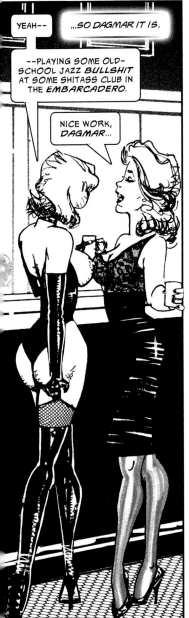

YEAH--

...SO DAGMAR IT IS.

--PLAYING SOME OLD-SCHOOL JAZZ BULLSHIT AT SOME SHITASS CLUB IN THE EMBARCADERO.

NICE WORK, DAGMAR...

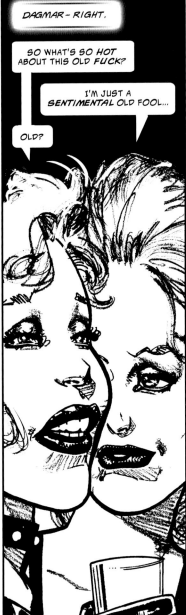

DAGMAR - RIGHT.

SO WHAT'S SO HOT ABOUT THIS OLD FUCK?

I'M JUST A SENTIMENTAL OLD FOOL...

OLD?

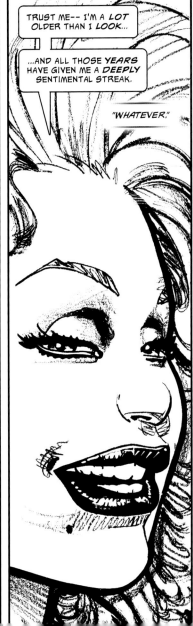

TRUST ME-- I'M A LOT OLDER THAN I LOOK...

...AND ALL THOSE YEARS HAVE GIVEN ME A DEEPLY SENTIMENTAL STREAK.

"WHATEVER."

SORRY ABOUT THAT SHIT WITH ROSEMARY.
NO PROBLEM.
FACT IS, YOU STILL FINDING ME FUCKABLE AT FORTY--
FORTY?
ALL RIGHT, FORTY-FIVE-
--INSTEAD OF THAT YOUNG BITCH--
--GETS ME SO SLICK I NEED A CHANGE OF PANTIES.
WHAT THE FUCK?
HEY, PAPI..
...FORGET THIS DRIED UP OLD CUNT...
...I DO THINGS WITH THIS MOUTH THAT'LL MAKE YOU MY BITCH.
TELL YOU WHAT-
--GET THE FUCK AWAY FROM ME RIGHT NOW, AND I WON'T CALL THE COPS.
DUDE, REALLY--
-YOU THINK BEVERLY GROVE GIVES A FUCK ABOUT COPS?

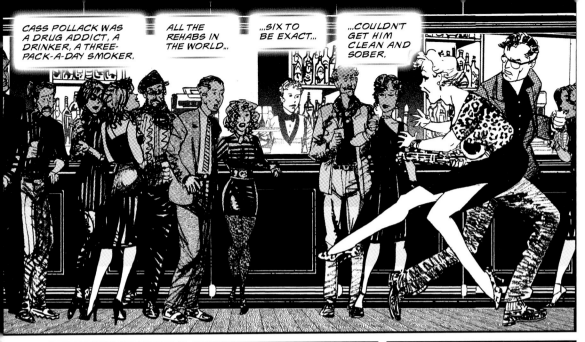

CASS POLLACK WAS A DRUG ADDICT, A DRINKER, A THREE-PACK-A-DAY SMOKER.

ALL THE REHABS IN THE WORLD...

...SIX TO BE EXACT...

...COULDN'T GET HIM CLEAN AND SOBER.

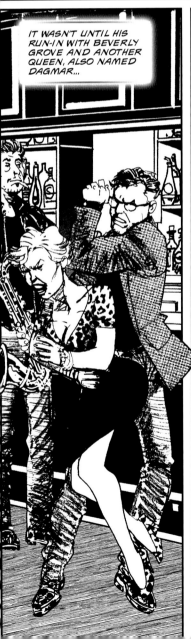

IT WASN'T UNTIL HIS RUN-IN WITH BEVERLY GROVE AND ANOTHER QUEEN, ALSO NAMED DAGMAR...

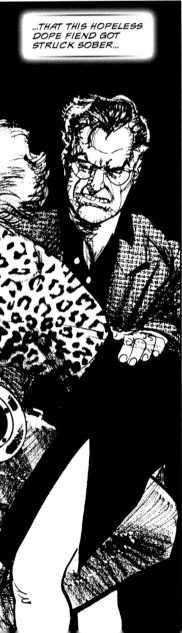

...THAT THIS HOPELESS DOPE FIEND GOT STRUCK SOBER...

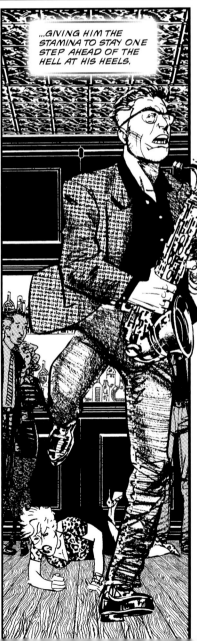

...GIVING HIM THE STAMINA TO STAY ONE STEP AHEAD OF THE HELL AT HIS HEELS.

BUT ALL GOOD THINGS COME TO AN END.
BEEN WONDERIN' WHEN YOU'D GET HOME...
...'S' YOU CAN SEE...
...I GOT TIRED OF WAITING.
WHO THE FUCK'RE YOU?
WHO GIVES A SHIT, CASS?
HE JUST BEAT THE SHIT OUT OF ME, THEN RAPED ME...
...KILL THIS MOTHERFUCKER, MAN.
SHUT THE FUCK UP, YOU LITTLE WHORE.
YOU CAN DO IT.

NOT BEFORE YOU GO FIRST, CUNT.
YOU NEXT, FAGGOT?
GAH...
THAT'S RIGHT, COME AND GET IT.
UNGGGCCCHHH-!
NOT SO TOUGH NOW, HUH, ASSHOLE?
SUCKER PUNCH ME, MOTHERFUCKER ...?

YOU GOT THE WEIGHT AND THE REACH, PAPI, BUT I GOT YOUTH ON MY SIDE.
WHAT'S WITH YOU AND THIS COCKSUCKER?
CASS...
...IT'S BEEN WAY TOO LONG.
WE HAVE REAL HISTORY, HE AND I.
YEAH, WELL, YOU'RE DONE WITH YOUR HISTORY...
...I WANT TO FUCK HIM UP GOOD.
WE'LL SEE, WE'LL SEE--
--LET'S NOT GET AHEAD OF OURSELVES.
SO WHERE'S MY MONEY?
THAT'S ALL YOU PEOPLE EVER THINK ABOUT, ISN'T IT?
NOW ALL WE DO IS MAKE THIS LOOK LIKE A LOVER'S TRIANGLE GONE BAD...
...WITH CASS HERE AS THE ACUTE ANGLE...
...AND WE ARE JUST GOLDEN.

End Chapter Eleven.

Spring, 2010...
...Southern California...
...Santa Varda, to be specific.
WHAT THE FUCK'RE WE *DOING* HERE?
HERE?
SANTA FUCKING *VARDA*, FOR FUCK'S SAKE.
FUCKING TOWN GOES TO SLEEP AT *NINE*, WAKES UP WITH THE FUCKING *CHICKENS*--
AND WHAT'S YOUR *POINT?*
MY POINT IS LIFE IS PASSING *ME*--
--*US*, BY.
I WANT A LITTLE *NIGHTLIFE*, A LITTLE *FUN* WHILE I'M *YOUNG*.
I *HATE* TO RUIN YOUR *DAY*, DAG--
--BUT YOU'RE *NOBODY'S* IDEA OF *YOUNG* ANYMORE.
FUCK *YOU*, KITTY, OR BEVERLY, OR CUNT FACE--
--*WHATEVER* THE FUCK YOUR NAME IS...

...I'M GOING BUGFUCK IN THIS ONE-HORSE SHITBURG.
NOT LIKE THE OLD DAYS, HUH, CASS?
I'D TELL DAGMAR TO JUMP...
YEAH--
--NEXT THING YOU KNOW, THERE'S A DRAG QUEEN WHO'S A DEAD RINGER FOR YOU...
...SPRAWLED AT THE BASE OF A TWENTY-STORY BUILDING IN A POOL OF HER OWN BLOOD.
YOU ALWAYS DID HAVE A SMART MOUTH ON YOU.
IT'S WHAT'S KEPT ME OUT OF THE BIG TIME FOR YEARS.
TAKE IT FROM ONE WHO KNOWS...
...THE BIG TIME IS TERRIBLY OVERRATED.
HAVING SPENT MY LIFE LOOKING AT IT FROM THE OUTSIDE, I WOULDN'T KNOW.
IF THERE'S ANYONE ALIVE WHO KNOWS MY STORY AND MY HISTORY, IT'S YOU, CASS, HONEY.
I'VE LIVED OVER A CENTURY, ON THE FRINGES OF FAME...
...AND ALL YOU GET FROM YOUR BIG TIME IS HIGHER EXPECTATIONS AND DEEPER DISAPPOINTMENT.

NONE OF THIS IS NEW TO CASS.
HE'S BEEN HEARING VARIATIONS ON THIS THEME FOR A DECADE.
THIS WOMAN...
...OR WHATEVER SHE IS OR MAY BE...
...OWNS HIS ANCIENT ASS, BODY AND SOUL.
AND IF THERE'S ANYTHING HE'S ACTUALLY GRATEFUL FOR IN THE EQUATION...
...IT'S THAT AT HIS AGE, IN HIS SHAPE...
...SHE HASN'T TRIED TO TURN HIM INTO THE NEXT DAGMAR...
WHATEVER YOU DO--
--PLEASE DON'T BITE IT OFF.

NEVER EVEN CROSSED MY MIND, DARLING...
...BUT NOW THAT YOU MENTION IT...
...DOESN'T THE FEAR I MIGHT GET YOU EVEN HOTTER?
...MOSTLY BECAUSE, HE SUSPECTS...
...HE'D MAKE AN UGLY WOMAN.
SHE'S GONE FROM VAUDEVILLE, TO SILENTS, TO TALKIES...
NOT EVEN A LITTLE.
...FROM CABARET TO NUDIES...
COULD'VE FOOLED ME, SWEETHEART...
...THAT DICK OF YOURS GOT HARDER THE MINUTE YOU MENTIONED IT.
AND SPEAKING OF HARD...

"...I NEED YOU TO DO A LITTLE SOMETHING FOR ME."
I WANT YOUR TONGUE UP MY ASS, BITCH...
...AND I MEAN NOW!
...AND SINCE HER RESURRECTION, EUNICE - ILONA - BLANCHE - BEVERLY - KITTY...
DO IT, SHARON...
...DO WHAT MISTRESS SAYS--
YEOOWW...!!
GO A LITTLE EASIER THERE, HUH?
...HAS BEEN RAKING IT IN ON THE INTERNET.
FUCK YOU, YOU WORTHLESS PIECE OF SHIT.
YOUR ASS IS MINE...
...AND YOUR ASSHOLE'S NOT AN EXIT ANYMORE.
THERE WAS A TIME IN HIS LIFE...
...TWENTY-FIVE, THIRTY YEARS AGO...
...WHEN THIS SORT OF ACTION, THIS SORT OF ROLE PLAYING...
...WAS CASS POLLACKS IDEA OF A PERFECT EVENING AT HOME.
TO NO ONE'S SURPRISE, THOSE DAYS ARE LONG GONE.

WHAT'RE YOU *WAITING* FOR, FISH?
SORRY, MISTRESS--
--I'LL DO BETTER *NEXT* TIME.
YOU DON'T DO AS YOU'RE *TOLD,* THERE WON'T *BE* A NEXT TIME.
MY CUM IS PURE *GOLD,* FISH CUNT...
...SO YOU BETTER GET *EVERY* DROP, IF YOU KNOW WHAT'S *GOOD* FOR YOU.
HIS *ASS...?*
I SAY YOU COULD *TALK?*
YOU SHOULD BE *GRATEFUL* YOU GET TO SUCK MY COCK *DRY...*
...AND LICK YOUR PISSANT *EXCUSE* FOR A HUSBAND'S *SHIT* OFF MY DICK, *TOO.*
WHAT'D I *SAY* ABOUT *GRATEFUL?*

THANK YOU, *MISTRESS.*
HA--
--I GOTTA GIVE YOU *CREDIT*--
--YOU GOT *SPIRIT,* FISH CUNT...
...AND YOU'VE GOT *TWICE* THE BALLS OF THIS MISERABLE *EXCUSE* FOR A MAN YOU CALL YOUR HUSBAND...
...RIGHT, YOU WASTE OF *PROTOPLASM?*
Mmmpphh...
JUST *NOD,* SHITSTAIN...
OKAY.
Snikk.

I NEED YOU BOTH TO PAY ATTENTION.
WHEN THE POLICE GET HERE, HERE'S THE STORY YOU'RE GOING TO GIVE THEM.
YOU WERE SITTING IN BED, READING, WHEN YOUR HOME WAS INVADED BY A TRIO OF MASKED CRIMINALS.
THEY RAPED BOTH OF YOU AT GUNPOINT, UNTIL ONE OF THEM, CLEARLY ON DRUGS, INADVERTANTLY KILLED HIS ACCOMPLICE HERE.
ARE WE CLEAR?
I SAID, ARE WE CLEAR?
YES.
YES, MASTER.
"MASTER?"
FOR CHRIST'S SAKE.
YOU'RE HARDLY IN ANY POSITION TO MOCK RITUAL AND FETISH, CASS...

WHATEVER YOU SAY.
QUESTION IS, NOW THAT YOU'VE DITCHED DAGMAR NUMBER WHATEVER...
...WHO'S NEXT IN LINE?
AND PLEASE, GOD, DON'T SAY IT'S ME.
YOU DO FLATTER YOURSELF, OLD MAN.
WE BOTH KNOW JUST HOW UGLY A WOMAN YOU'D MAKE.
BUT SERIOUSLY.
BUT SERIOUSLY...
...AS A THERAPIST MIGHT PUT IT...

...I THINK I'VE HAD A BREAKTHROUGH.
MEANING WHAT?
Kitty Litter XXX
Kitty Litter XXX
MEANING, AFTER EIGHTY YEARS AND FIVE DIFFERENT DAGMARS...
...I THINK I'VE MOVED ON...
...AND I CAN GET ALONG WITHOUT A TWIN.
...AND WHERE DO I STAND IN THIS, KITTY?
YOU'LL JUST KEEP WORKING FOR ME UNTIL YOU'RE TOO OLD...
...AT WHICH POINT I'LL GUT YOU, EAT YOU AND FIND SOMEONE NEW.
WILL YOU LOOK AT THAT?
THAT CRAZY BITCH COULD ROLE PLAY, DON'T YOU THINK?
THE END.

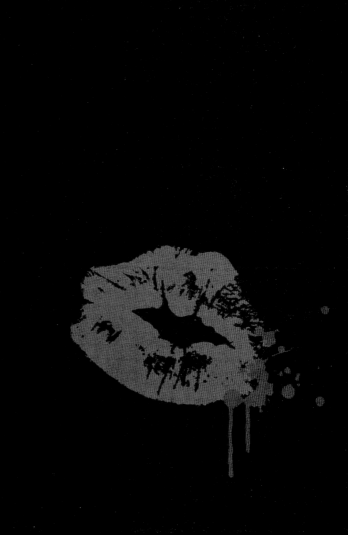

ALSO BY HOWARD CHAYKIN

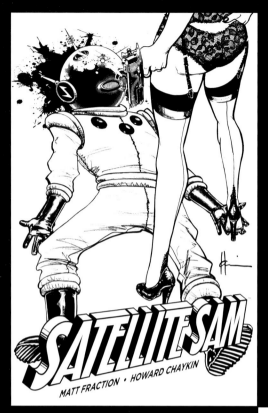

New York City 1951: The star of beloved daily television serial "Satellite Sam" turns up dead in a flophouse filled with dirty secrets. The police think it was death by natural causes, but his son knows there was something more... if only he could sober up long enough to do something about it. This noir mystery shot through with sex and violence exposes the seedy underbelly of the golden age of television.

Century, Texas used to be a sleepy little burg, barely a whistlestop between nowhere and the great beyond... until the 20th Century arrived with a bang, bringing with it automobiles, aeroplanes, telephones, paved streets... and, of course, the movies.

Howard Chaykin tells the colorful story of the American West, transformed from frontier to legend, and how the American dream became a modern myth.

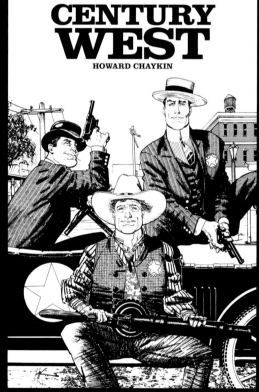